A WORLD OF DIFFERENCE
THE BIG GREEN POETRY MACHINE

Poems From The UK And Around The World

Edited by Lisa Adlam & Genya Beeby

First published in Great Britain in 2009 by:

Young Writers

Young Writers
Remus House
Coltsfoot Drive
Peterborough
PE2 9JX
Telephone: 01733 890066
Website: www.youngwriters.co.uk
All Rights Reserved
Book Design by Ali Smith & Tim Christian
© Copyright Contributors 2008
SB ISBN 978-1-84431-934-3

Foreword

Young Writers' Big Green Poetry Machine is a showcase for our nation's most brilliant young poets to share their thoughts, hopes and fears for the planet they call home.

Young Writers was established in 1991 to nurture creativity in our children and young adults, to give them an interest in poetry and an outlet to express themselves. Seeing their work in print will encourage them to keep writing as they grow, and become our poets of tomorrow.

Selecting the poems has been challenging and immensely rewarding. The effort and imagination invested by these young writers makes their poems a pleasure to enjoy reading time and time again.

Contents

Eleanor Manley (9)	1
Brittany Buttle (8)	2
Suku Ncube (9)	3
Kezia Niman (9)	4
Emily Siva (9) & Melanie Colbey (9)	5
Jake Silverstone & Martin Wassmer (9)	6
Ella Inwald & Rotem Reske (9)	7
Danielle Isaacs (9)	8
Mia Whitefield & Dana Nitzani (9)	9
Ben Karsberg & Joss Bogod (9)	10
Sam Brown & Jacob Arbeid (9)	11
Shira Shimansky (8)	12
Joshua Aaron Daniels & Daniel Philip Janowski (9)	13
Oscar Kraft (9)	14
Lydia Brady (9)	15
Louis Brady (8)	16
Olivia Kersey (10)	17
Andi Marsh (9)	18
Imogen Alison Squire (8)	19
Mereida Fajardo (8)	20
Orla McArthur (8)	21
Christopher Cox (10)	22
Ellie Louise Waite (10)	23
Emily Whittemore (8)	24
Saffran Harrington (8)	25
Amy Elizabeth Knowles (8)	26
Stevie Stanton (11)	27
Tansy Lewis (11)	28
Rowan Keith (11)	29
Charity Ellis (11)	30
Finn Areki (7)	31
Izzy Roan (9)	32
Calum Lewis (9)	33
Mark Morgan (9)	34
Alex Hawtin (9)	35
Sam Bell (9)	36
Jamie Banning (9)	37
Laura Morrison (9)	38
William Hoque (9)	39
George Bayley (9)	40
Jake Ward (9)	41
Poppy Ward (8)	42
Rachael Taylor (10)	43
Guy Finch (9)	44
Oliver Hague (10)	45
Holly Upshall (10)	46
Matthew Cooke (10)	47
Emily Robins (10)	48
Emma Hodgson (10)	49
Emily Booker (10)	50
Toby Jarrett (10)	51
Gabrielle Katie Pybus (10)	52
India Lewis (10)	53
Chloe Lauren Parker (9)	54
Rory Walder (10)	55
Jessica Simpson (10)	56
Dominic Tarrant (10)	57
Jordan Wilks (8)	58
Paige Featherstone (8)	59
Philip Parkin-Swain (7)	60
Thomas Breslin (8)	61
Holly Keys (8)	62
Max Stevens (7)	63
Charlie Lee Jaques (10)	64
Reece Puckett (10)	65
Georgina Norman (11)	66
Freddie Livermore (10)	67
Priscilla Okyere-Davko (10)	68
Grace Harrington (7)	69
Adam Bailey (7)	70
Georgina Johnson (7)	71
Rosie Grant (7)	72
Lily Clarke (7)	73
Kelly Jayne Alexander (10)	74
Aaron Reilly (10)	75
James Smith (10)	76
Canan Djouma (9)	77
Logan Walby-Williams (9)	78
Steven King (9)	79
Robert Seaman (9)	80
Kelly Walsh (9)	81
Sam Key (9)	82
Taylor Wild (9)	83
Anya Herd (8)	84
George Sexton (8)	85
Victoria Wilson (8)	86
Nathan Wilby (8)	87
Maddie Leeds (7)	88
Jasmin Deb (8)	89
Kade Presland (8)	90
Rebecca Sparrow (8)	91
Mason Johnson (7)	92

Nadine Bakali (8)	93
Rikki-Leigh Carr (8)	94
Ryan Needs (8)	95
Ellis Richardson (10)	96
Lucy Sween (7)	97
Shannon Walby-Williams (7)	98
Jamie Amatruda (7)	99
Zara Masood (8)	100
Haydn Brooks (9)	101
Daisy Green (9)	102
Eloise Hadley (9)	103
Jacob Haycox (9)	104
Jason Bond (8)	105
Megan Fordham (9)	106
Nikita Dheer (9)	107
Nilum Mistry (9)	108
Hannah Thompson (9)	109
Alicia Carey (9)	110
Emily Costello (9)	111
Paige James (9)	112
Lauren Morgan (9)	113
Savannah Carter (9)	114
Jordan Pocknell (9)	115
Eva Basnett (9)	116
Caitlin Carr (8)	117
Ashley Bodycote (9)	118
Rebecca Hartopp (9)	119
Georgia Sian Porter (9)	120
Divian Mistry (9)	121
Trafford Warwick (9)	122
Thomas Carter (9)	123
Bradley Matthew Garratt (9)	124
Oliver Haslam (9)	125
Robert Rice (9)	126
Sam Baldwin (11)	127
India Hutchason (11)	128
Nathan Browne (10)	129
Emma Sankey (10)	130
Dominic Bowler (11)	131
Yasmin Butler (10)	132
Rowan Heaton (10)	133
Eve Procter (10)	134
Ben Cooper (10)	135
Oliver Thompson (10)	136
Luke Baskerville (10)	137
Callum Makepeace (10)	138
Bethany Kitching (10)	139
Lauren Shepherdson (11)	140
Laura Yaxley (11)	141
Matthew Wilson (10)	142
Brooke Kelsey (11)	143
Sylvie Wilkinson (11)	144
Hazel Richardson (10)	145
Olivia Beckham (10)	146
Mayson Banforth (10)	147
Victoria Hazlegreaves (10)	148
Ali Tabet (10)	149
Michael Kearns (10)	150
Clemens Weileder (10)	151
Catherine Watts (10)	152
Laura Henao Hernandez (11)	153
Jack Beaton (10)	154
Adam Yasir (10)	155
James Hawthorn (11)	156
Rebecca Wood (10)	157
Jessica Brough (11)	158
Maria Bukley (11)	159
Oliver Beckham (11)	160
Danick Fritz Tchangou-Ngadjieu (8)	161
Lillie Makepeace (9)	162
Natalie Swan (9), Ashton & Harry	163
Ellie Hitt (9), Cleo & Oliver	164
Kimberley Walker (9) & Ashley	165
Joseph Scott (9) & Samantha	166
Eleanor Johnson (9)	167
Amber Goodsell-Collett (10)	168
Katie Wells (11)	169
Bethany Duncan-Skinner (11)	170
Sherie McCormick (11)	171
Chloe Wooldridge (11)	172
Hayley Hughes (11)	173
Daisy Houlan (11)	174
Hannah Eldridge (11)	175
Alice Taylor (11)	176
Megan Goee (11)	177
Ben Robinson (11)	178
Kayleigh Denman (11)	179
Finley Smith (9)	180
Charlotte Adams (9)	181
Sarah Thompson (9)	182
Harrison Jackson (9)	183
Isabella Goodwin (9)	184
Jasmine Northen (9)	185
Felicia Secker (9)	186
Alicia Shearsmith (9)	187
Emily Kirk (9)	188
Samuel Mahon (9)	189
Nadine Crofts (9)	190
Lee Hannath (9)	191
Laura Cunningham (9)	192

William Russell (9) 193
Alayna Johnson (9) 194
Megan Reynolds (9) 195
Harvey Mason (9) 196
Charlotte Perrin (9) 197
Jack Rayner (11) 198
Rosie Cook (8) 199
Christopher Evans (8) 200
Bradley Hemming (11) 201
Kieran Wilkins (11) 202
Georgia Hughes (11) 203
Catrin Thomas (11) 204
Joshua Wheeler (11) 205
Toby McDowell (11) 206
Laura Hunt (11) 207
Alex Rodgers (11) 208
Amelia Andrews (11) 209
Adam Bassett (11) 210
Charlotte Bourne (11) 211
Naomi Quoroll (11) 212
Stephen Ingarfield (11) 213
Joseph Robins (11) 214
Emma Gilpin (11) 215
Natasha Rega-Jones (11) 216
Daniel Buck (11) 217
Lucy Smallwood (11) 218
Sam Rollit (11) 219
Joseph Phee (11) 220
Rebecca Hunter (11) 221
Rebecca Pilot (11) 222

The Poems

Summer

The sun is so hot, the water so cool
Everyone is getting in the pool
Splashing about having some fun
Playing with a water gun
The smell of the barbeque is so good
We jump up in delight and eat our food
Then we need something to cool us down
The ice cream man is coming round
We run to the van to get our delight
Then it is back to the water fight.

Troy Fryer (8)

God Put You Here

God put you here, not to pick and choose,
To obey and act well, not to lie and abuse.
God gave you a mind not to leave alone,
To make this Earth a temporary home.
God gave you freedom, not to throw away,
To submit to Him and refrain from going astray.
God made cattle and plants for you,
Made them lawful to eat, all but a few.
God gave you manners and morality,
To practise them with much dignity.
God gave you sight, not to be blind,
To see with it and enlighten your mind.
God gave you hearing, not to ignore,
To seek knowledge and learn some more.
God gave you wisdom and good health,
To take care of His creatures, with plenty of strength,
God sent down His justice to make life fair,
But you turned away and did not care.

God put you here, not to pick and choose,
To obey and act well, not to lie and accuse.
God gave you and I the chance to know
How we were made and how we grow.
God put us here for a limited time,
Not to continuously indulge in crime.
God gave us tongues, limbs, hands and feet,
To rush to our friends and peacefully greet.
God made us in tribes and many nations,
To know and reflect upon all His creations.
God gave us a desire to be clean
And a natural inclination not to be mean.
God gave us power, status and might
Not to chase away citizens full of fright.
God gave us a life, a wonderful gift,
To encourage and motivate, to really uplift.
God sent down guidance to increase our good deeds,
But we are turning away and not taking heed.

Rukhsar Ahmed (15)
Al-Hijrah Secondary School, Birmingham

Just Me. Me And My Sister

One day, as I am sitting, sitting on the cold, damp kerb,
In the busy high street, just me and my sister,
Watching the snobby rich people go by,
We watch them stop and stare at our scruffy hair and scruffy clothes,
They stare at me, me and my sister.

Then someone takes pity,
Pity on me. Me and my sister, with our scruffy clothes,
They give £5.00, just enough to buy bread and a drink,
For me. Me and my sister.

We sit and wait, wait for our mum,
She doesn't come for me,
For me. Me and my sister.

An old abandoned shed,
Take off our tattered rucksacks
And wrap ourselves up,
Just me. Me and my sister.

We wake up to a loud bang,
It's the police, they have bad news,
Mum got caught stealing,
For me. Me and my sister.

So now we are in care,
We get new clothes and food every day,
We even get money,
So we don't have to steal food or beg.
Life is good, for me. Me and my sister.

Micaela-Lorraine Boyce (12)
All Saints Catholic College, Dukinfield

Green Life

Too many nuclear arms
We are destroying all the farms
To keep the grass nice and bright
Let's stop the fight
Help the trees grow
Stop making them go.

Francis Lloyd (11)
All Saints Catholic College, Dukinfield

Green, Green Grass

If only the grass was green
Like the big green poetry machine
If only the sky were blue
All just for me and you
If only people could see the world like we do
Then the world would be the better place we knew
If we all stop putting the world to waste
And all try to make it a better place.

Rachael Baker (12)
All Saints Catholic College, Dukinfield

Untitled

Smoke and emissions are coming out of our cars
We are going to end up just like Mars!
Our planet is boiling
Just like the fires on our sun.
Our polar caps are crumbling
Our cities are tumbling!

If we don't do something soon
We will all go boom!

Ryan Connor (12)
All Saints Catholic College, Dukinfield

A World Of Difference -Poems From The UK And Around The World

Changing The World

Stop litter,
Because it's bitter,
Stop the world from being mean,
By keeping it tidy and clean.
Try and stop the rain
And keep the animals out of pain.

Katie Dewsbury (12)
All Saints Catholic College, Dukinfield

The Green, Green World

Rubbish, rubbish everywhere
Make a difference to what you wear
Recycle, recycle your plastic bags
Recycle your old clothes
All that rubbish covering the Earth
It's like a big bin bag
That's bringing all the rats and cats out.

Recycle, recycle is what you need to do
That is a poem from the Big Green Poetry Machine.

Michaela Lovell (11)
All Saints Catholic College, Dukinfield

Stop Pollution

Pollution is bad
Pollution makes me mad
Please, stop pollution
We need a solution
It pollutes the Earth
The Earth could die
Sometimes it makes you cry
The cars make the pollution
We need to stop the cars
They really are as dark
As the polluted sky
So help us
Stop pollution!

Jack O'Neill
All Saints Catholic College, Dukinfield

The Humid Rainforest

In a humid rainforest, the sun shining so bright,
The birds singing in the middle of the night.
The beavers swimming in the river
Looking for some food,
As if the world was not so cruel.

I wonder if this day will last
But all I can think about is trash.
We should stop pollution,
We should start a revolution.

If you like your grass clean,
You should try to be more green,
If you try to be more green
Then the world will be clean.

Charlie Holland (12)
All Saints Catholic College, Dukinfield

A World Of Difference - Poems From The UK And Around The World

Where Have All The Polar Bears Gone?

Where have all the polar bears gone?
What is the world I have come from?
Is it a world full of monsters and beasts?
Why can't we all just have peace?

Why do we have to pollute Earth?
I wish I didn't have to walk on this turf,
Because we are killing the polar bears,
What have they done wrong, the poor little bears?

The ice caps are melting and turning to water,
The life of polar bears is getting shorter.
Oh why can't we save those bears?
Does no one on this Earth care?

Katie Howard (12)
All Saints Catholic College, Dukinfield

The Earth's Nightmare

The Earth is warming up day by day,
The ozone layer is being chipped away.
But still we cut down trees and use leaded fuel,
What we're doing to this planet is oh so cruel.

Why must we travel everywhere in a car?
Even when we're not going far.
The animals of the world are affected too,
They'll vanish off the face of the Earth,
From the eyes of me and you.

The signs of the world heating up are there,
Floods, storms, droughts, cyclones, things we can hardly bear.
The plants and animals of the Earth vanishing away -
This environmental disaster will come true one day. . .

Robert John Flynn (12)
All Saints Catholic College, Dukinfield

Endangered

Think of a world without any bears,
Global warming will give them nightmares.
Magnificent creatures
Are the world's features
Some are about to go.

Global warming
Is a warning
To me and you
Recycle is the thing to do.

Leatherback turtles can easily go
If we stop hunting you and me know
They can make a comeback
The turtle numbers will not lack.

Alex Barker (12)
All Saints Catholic College, Dukinfield

War

Why is there war?
What do we need it for?
It takes too many lives,
The pain we get inside.

The horrific pain of war,
What do we need it for?
All the things destroyed, each and every day
Even if we try it will not fade away.

Families losing loved ones
For no particular cause
Why does it have to happen?
Couldn't we just press pause?

Just for a moment of silence
Just for a moment of peace
Can't we have a rest from it
And make it all cease?

The piercing sound of bullets
Flashing by
If they hit you
They'll make you cry.

The piercing sensation
Passing through the flesh
Once I heard it's like
A knife ripping through mesh.

Why is there war?
What do we need it for?
It takes too many lives,
The pain we get inside.

George Richardson (11)
All Saints Catholic College, Dukinfield

Horrible War

War is horrible,
War is cruel,
All the killers
Are just big fools.
Missiles flying
Through the air,
Families dying,
But they don't care!
Thousands dropping,
Just like flies.
All you can hear
Are the families' cries.
So at the end of the day,
War is wrong.
Why can't we all
Just get along?

Daniel Fraidoon-Pour (12)
All Saints Catholic College, Dukinfield

Pollution Problems

There's black, green and grey,
It should be sunny, it's May.
Too many cars driving around,
Petrol gone up a few pound.
Fumes all around, in the air,
From cars, trains and planes.
It's a shame, no one has a care,
The Earth isn't green anymore.
The skies aren't blue,
Apples rotting down to the core.
The ozone layer fading away,
It's too hot, now it's May.

Sophie Pemberton (12)
All Saints Catholic College, Dukinfield

War

W hen will you stop fighting?
A re you aware you are damaging family homes?
R uining people's lives - scared for their lives.

W hat is the point of fighting?
A lot of people hurt, damaging members of a family.
R ealise that a lot of living area is getting damaged.

Cameron McDonald (11)
All Saints Catholic College, Dukinfield

War

Why are you obsessed with war?
Why are we obsessed with war?
Why is humanity obsessed with war?

Because of our differences . . .
Because of our beliefs . . .
Because of our opinions . . .

Why do they need to die?
Why do they need to suffer?
What does it accomplish?

More war . . .

Simon Kenworthy (12)
All Saints Catholic College, Dukinfield

Cruelty To Animals

A nimals are being wiped out
N o one can stop the hunter's clout
I n the world hunters are everywhere
M any hunters are unfair
A hunter kills animals, from rabbits to bears
L ying in a black market, where hunters make their profit
S o come on people, let's stop it!

Alexander Colton (11)
All Saints Catholic College, Dukinfield

Racism

I wanna go home
Why do they hurt me?
Please!

Sticks and stones
May break my bones
But bullies cannot harm me.

They mock
They punch
Oh please, press pause
I'm desperate!

Just a helpless child
Praying for glory
Hear my prayers!

Levi Robertson (11)
All Saints Catholic College, Dukinfield

No Hope

P oor
O ur problem
V ery hungry
E very person for themselves
R eality
T ime ticking by
Y our problem

Poverty is our problem
Without your help there is
No water, no food, no hope . . .

Alice Storey (12)
All Saints Catholic College, Dukinfield

Little Fishes

Deep down below the water
Supplies are going to get shorter,
Our little fishes
Are going to end up on our dishes.
We need to stop this madness,
So we can live in happiness.

Victoria Ormrod (12)
All Saints Catholic College, Dukinfield

Pollution

P ollution is destroying the ozone layer
O ur world is getting hotter and hotter
L et's help reduce pollution
L anzarote is what England will be in 10 years
U nless we do something about it
T he litter and smoke are making pollution
I am helping reduce the amount of litter
O n the planet some people are helping out
N ow please, you help save the world.

Evan Russell (11)
All Saints Catholic College, Dukinfield

Disasters In The World

Swing, swing from tree to tree
There's more water coming to the sea
It's droughts here and floods there
And down there there's a grizzly bear.

Days and nights are going
But sadly it's still not snowing
Hotter and hotter the world gets
But the sun's brave, because it still sets.

The animals are weaker and starting to die
But no one can help them, why?
Their feet and hands are getting sore
So please don't use petrol anymore.

Atlanta Mistry-Wardle (12)
All Saints Catholic College, Dukinfield

Environment

E very animal counts
N o one should kill them
V ery many trees are being cut down
I cebergs are melting fast
O ut there polar bears are dying
N oisy trucks fill the air
M any fumes can kill a bear
E lephants are being hunted for their tusks
N ow is the time to act
T he world is changing.

Ciaran Beswick (12)
All Saints Catholic College, Dukinfield

Planet Problems

Trees are getting chopped down
It's not funny, not like a clown,
The environment is getting polluted.
It is just not suited,
Animals are dying out,
It's really time for you to pout.
It's really time to save our planet,
Do it, don't just plan it!
We should all be recycling,
Before the world blows up and goes *bang!*
Which everyone will see.
Everyone who is starting to litter
Makes the rain go patter-pitter.

Jenna Turner (12)
All Saints Catholic College, Dukinfield

My Disappearing World

Tigers are going,
Rivers might stop flowing,
Rhinos too,
What are we to do?

Elephants are under threat,
Some are caught with a net,
Parrots are going fast,
The blue whales will never last.

Do you want your grandchildren to see
A red squirrel in a tree?
Save the animals, fast,
Or they'll be in the past.

Jenny Martin (12)
All Saints Catholic College, Dukinfield

Save The Rainforests

Rainforests belong to the birds and bees,
But we're destroying their homes,
For paper which comes from the trees.

But some of these animals are close to becoming extinct,
So we have to do something,
We have to think.

We can recycle our paper, recycle today,
Do it now and save the rainforests,
Or these animals will pay.

Lewis Boulton (12)
All Saints Catholic College, Dukinfield

Rainforest

If you listen to my poem today,
You'll know we're to pay,
Those birds, it's their habitat,
They don't live with us, like a cat.
So stop cutting down their trees,
Or you'll be on your knees.
All those bugs, monkeys, wonderful things,
Just to show what life brings.
If you want to know how,
Just recycle your paper, now!

Hannah Welsh (12)
All Saints Catholic College, Dukinfield

Deforestation

Rainforests used to be all over this world,
But now they've been destroyed by machines that whirled and curled.
The animals are killed with no mercy,
Most are now hungry and thirsty.
Don't let the future nation
Suffer with deforestation.
Stand up and recycle
And ride to school on a bicycle.

Harry Whewell (12)
All Saints Catholic College, Dukinfield

Our World

Recently our world
Has been flipped, turned and twirled,
We've ruined our atmosphere,
Which has caused a lot of fear.
We are harming millions of animals,
Such as reptiles, birds and many mammals.
Maybe this world could turn
If we all attempted to learn.
A world that is no longer a messy place,
But a world to live life with the rest of the human race.

Charlotte Knight (12)
All Saints Catholic College, Dukinfield

The Dark Planet

Every morning
There could be global warming
Factories giving off smoke
Making the ozone layer choke.

We have to save the planet
So everyone should go manic
Cutting down a tree
Is making the planet worse for me.

The snow is melting fast
The world won't last
The water is overflowing
But people aren't knowing.

We should listen to the news
And look for clues
The planet is dying fast
So let's help the planet last.

Lewis Davies (11)
All Saints Catholic College, Dukinfield

Nature

N o one cares about nature
A nimals are dying
T oucans are squawking
U gly things happening
R acoons are being tortured
E veryone who does this is disgraceful.

James Garside (12)
All Saints Catholic College, Dukinfield

Saving Our Friend

Earth, our friend, our mother, our life
But is this how we treat friends?
Bid them to annihilation.
Death! Destruction! Weakening every day.

Her forests burnt!
The atmosphere contaminated!
Temperatures rising! Resources wasted!
Selfishness rules our decisions,
Like a small child,
Without a thought for anyone but I!

Climate change!
Food shortages, no fuel!
That is what we doing to our friend.
Yet, she patiently, waits for us to change our ways.
But time is running out,
Our lives are slowly swallowing our dearest friend.

Many of us turning a blind eye
To more sustainable solutions.
Wind energy, solar energy?
Even walking instead of driving.
But it starts with one person changing their habits;
Picking litter instead of throwing it.

Selflessly considering the future,
It is not that difficult.
But remember, time is against us,
We need to act quickly and save our friend!

Pamela Hoto (14)
Arundel School, Zimbabwe

A Solution for Pollution

The trees are dying
And the grass is no longer green.
What happened to our home; the Earth,
That once used to be clean?
The beaches are filthy
And the ocean is full of debris and cans,
The fish are dying
And this is all because of our very own men.
The sky is no longer clear,
It's full of pollution.
Maybe if we stop using as much gas,
That'll be a solution.

Brittany Patrice Smith (16)
Bermuda Institute, Bermuda

Tree

Wood supplier
Shade maker
Home giver
Helpless viewer
Prime target
Oldest friend
Approaching end
Plant many!

Chelsea Crockwell (16)
Bermuda Institute, Bermuda

She Cries

She cries out for help
her heart is dying
the tears of her sorrow
fall more and more
flooding the hopes of tomorrow

Her fury is known,
she shouts, she's mad
she moans and groans
she asks for help in an unusual way
sighing with a constant rhythm
that interrupts the stillness of the day

All she wants is for someone to care
being used is something she feels is not fair
all she wants is nourishment
pick up the trash
recycle your mess
don't use unnecessary things with excess
only buy what you need
use less gas
be a good sport and my fury will be in the past.

Samara Wilson (14)
Bermuda Institute, Bermuda

Trees

Big, green
Chop down
Make frown
Please don't
Oxygen needed
Can't breathe
Crying out
Save me!

Mikayla Deshields (14)
Bermuda Institute, Bermuda

Environment

E verybody must
N ot smoke
V iolence
I n security
R ecycle
O n Tuesdays
N ot any other day
M ake the
E nvironment full of
N ature and
T rees.

Jake Mills
Bishop's College, Gloucester

The Environment

When I used to think of the environment,
I thought of no pollution, no rubbish,
No global warming and nature and life living happily.
But now I think of dead trees and lots of pollution,
The humankind want to change it, they won't leave the world alone,
Nothing will tone,
We all believe
That one day we will be no more.

Luke Richards (12)
Bishop's College, Gloucester

Every Little Helps

The trees are green,
Turning brown,
Together we can
Do this.
Let's take these litterbugs down.
We can make these people happy,
We can wipe off their frown.

Josh Hergest
Bishop's College, Gloucester

Animal Cages

We don't hear them in their cages,
We can't see the pain;
They are so replaceable,
We may as well treat them sickly.
We force dangerous acids down their throats,
They are so replaceable.
Why put make-up on monkeys?
Why see how long kittens last?
For they are *not* replaceable,
Their souls cannot strive to rest.
Crying for the animals,
What can that do?
So something about it,
They depend on you.

Claudia Taylor (13)
Bishop's Hatfield Girls' School, Hatfield

Recycle

Recycle the glass
Recycle the plastic
Make this world look fantastic

Recycle the paper
Recycle the plastic
Make this world look fantastic

Recycle the cardboard
Recycle the plastic
Make this world look fantastic

Recycle the bags
Recycle the plastic
Make this world look fantastic
Make this world look extra fantastic.

Emma-Louise Ingrey (13)
Bishop's Hatfield Girls' School, Hatfield

Recycle

Use less paper,
Don't be a waster,
Don't be dim,
Recycle your tin.

Global warming,
Nature's warning.

Turn out the light
If it's not night.
Don't make a fuss,
Get the bus.

Global warming,
Nature's warning.

Don't use the car
If it's not that far.
Recycle paper,
It will be used later.

Global warming,
Nature's warning.

Bethany Peters (13)
Bishop's Hatfield Girls' School, Hatfield

Don't Litter

There is rubbish on the floor
And then once more.
This is litter,
Really bitter.
I don't agree.

It should not be,
It can't be true,
To blame you.
Don't do it,
It's not worth it.

Don't litter,
It's bitter.
Don't do it,
Pick it up!

Emily Coates (13)
Bishop's Hatfield Girls' School, Hatfield

Starving On The Streets

Children are starving on the streets
We have lots of food to eat
Don't waste your rubbish, don't throw it in the bin
You never know, it may be committing a sin.

Starvation and hunger give you a clue
To help you understand what you could do
Every day we live and learn
On what could *you* spend the money *you* earn?

Take a moment to look inside
Think of the starving children you could help worldwide.

Madeleine Tavner (13)
Bishop's Hatfield Girls' School, Hatfield

Bang

Bang go the guns, night and day
Nothing really to say
Only that people are dying
For human rights
And all they do is fight and fight
So let people die, so let people fly
But only to hit the ground
And at the end
There won't be a sound
Because nothing will be left
Just think of the people at home
Waiting at the phone
For a call from their loved ones
So just think of the pain
Think of the hatred
But only one thing can be said
People are fighting for the world's tomorrow
So we can have a better life
So give them respect
For a world we have not seen
But they have seen too soon.

Emma Bethany Johansen (13)
Bishop's Hatfield Girls' School, Hatfield

Some Animals Are Extinct

Some animals are extinct
So I'm going to make you think
Tigers, elephants and pandas are dying
This is so bad we should be crying
All the animals are going
This is why I wrote this poem.

Shannon Davies (13)
Bishop's Hatfield Girls' School, Hatfield

My Friend, The Tree

I stand tall above the ground,
When the wind blows I make a sound,
You climb upon me every day,
When all of the children come out to play.
I am one of your best friends
And I will be until the end,
But one day you came out to play,
Your best friend was being cut away.
The roaring of the monster that cut down your friend
Was loud and violent and would never end.
But you came back another day
And planted a seed that grew away,
Big and tall it grew and grew,
A new best friend for me and you . . .

Melissa Mountford (13)
Bishop's Hatfield Girls' School, Hatfield

Power Of Poverty

Where can you go where the poor are no more?
Where can you go where people don't beg at the door?
How long will it take to stop starvation
And stand up as a nation and say 'No more?'

Laura Aldridge (13)
Bishop's Hatfield Girls' School, Hatfield

Our Earth

The Earth is ours to enjoy
For every little girl and boy.
But we must always be aware
That this Earth needs a bit of care.
With all the children yet to come,
Who want to play and laugh and run,
Around the trees and in the garden.
So we must keep our planet free
Of messy trash, from you and me.
To keep the air fresh and clear,
For all to breathe from year to year.
We must never, ever abuse
This place that's here for us to use.

Laura Butler (12)
Bishop's Hatfield Girls' School, Hatfield

The Country

I lie there, in the grass,
Gazing up at the blazing blue bowl, scattered with clouds.
I hear the trees swaying, their leaves shining like gold,
I smell the fresh sweet hay, gazed down upon by an incandescent sun.
The fresh air tastes like a sweet apple, soothing and refreshing.
But however, not sour like the air of a polluted city,
The natural grass has a perpetual glow, like the glow of a hearty angel.

This heaven can be visited regularly, it is known as the country.

Thomas Gray (15)
Borden Grammar School, Sittingbourne

The Saxon Shore Way Walk

The Saxon Shore Way, it's soft gentle flow,
Meandering, winding, breezing.

From urban roar
To sweet-sounding scenes.

The creek lies below
When tide is low,
The seabirds do gather,
Together they fall and together they rise.

The Saxon Shore Way, it's strong-scented stench
Filling the air and filling my path.

To industrial might, to industrial waste,
Pollution builds with haste.

The Saxon Shore Way with nature amongst,
Preserve, protect, progress.

Joe White (15)
Borden Grammar School, Sittingbourne

Industrial Britain

In the distance a chimney
Pours out its thick black smoke.
Rolling like a landslide,
Covering up the sun.
The men
Walking in and out,
Black as the coal they've worked with.

Next to me, a man,
Unclean and unkempt,
His ragged clothes filthy,
His hair long and thin,
His cheeks are sunken in,
His eyes are red raw.
Out of a job, alone on the streets,
No food, no money, not a place to stay.
I say to myself, I would sooner die
Than live a life worth nothing at all.

Then I hear it,
The clashing of hooves
On the stone road beside me.
I look, I see,
A horse,
Proud and magnificent,
Its coat shining white,
It eyes a deep black.
On top,
A rider,
His clothes are of
Good quality and fabric,
The colours clashing,
Dark red and bright yellow.
His well-fed face,
His hair,
Well cut
And gleaming.

He sits
Atop his horse,
Not looking around him,
Thinking himself above
These troubles and sufferings.

Joseph Doney (15)
Borden Grammar School, Sittingbourne

YoungWriters

Our Once Proud Nation

Broken bottles, used cigarettes,
This is a land full of regrets.
Wasting it all, upon every corner,
Wasting it all, just for a laugh.

Rubbish, food, guarding the floor,
Plenty of food to feed all the poor.
Our pride and honour has all disappeared,
Our once proud nation now kicked up the rear.

Broken beer bottles and a big pub brawl,
Between immature pigs, who *need* to look cool.
Used to be tea with two sugars or more
And the cleanest nation one ever saw.
Now all that remains is dirt and disgrace,
As beer and violence bring nothing but pain!

Our flag now;
Tattered, battered, shattered and scattered,
As if anyone thinks now, that any of that matters . . .

Ryan Gorman
Borden Grammar School, Sittingbourne

London Underground

Down, down, down,
Merging into the darkness,
Lights flashing past me,
The enclosed smell drifts from every station,
The feeling of worthlessness surrounds everyone,
Every beggar asking for sympathy,
The sudden rush of the Devil's barge,
Then a mad dash for the entrance to Hell.
The sweaty coffin finally pulls away,
The sudden jolt of a fellow sufferer,
An immediate rush to reach the light,
To find yourself concealed at your desk.

Lewis Charlesworth (15)
Borden Grammar School, Sittingbourne

Simply Cricket

The toss of a silver coin will decide,
The decision of to bat or to field,
Whites, gentlemen in uniform,
Eleven stand on the lovingly kept, emerald-green grass.
The batsman steps from the pavilion,
Walks to the crease,
Takes his guard and prepares for the first ball.
The bowler, composed,
Sprints in from his mark and delivers the red-stitched cannon ball,
The fielders wait with eager anticipation.
Chasing the forever rolling sphere,
The constant knock of the ball to bat,
With the cry of *'Howzat!'*
The umpire shakes his head in his all white robe,
He signals for tea when the over has closed.
The spread of sandwiches, cheese and cucumber,
Cakes and grapes.

Bradleigh Barrett (14)
Borden Grammar School, Sittingbourne

Memories Of A Beach

The suncream smeared on my sun-kissed body,
The water enveloping me as I swim in the open sea.

Millions of tiny missiles ready to be launched,
Competition heightened furthest, highest or skimmed.

The sun dries my body, a cold drink moistens my lips,
Hunger creeps up until we beat it no longer.

Our favourite fish and chips, so simple,
Yet the taste limitless, unique, traditional.

The batter crispy, the fish flaky, melts in your mouth,
Freshly caught,
The chips not too soft, a crisp texture to the exterior.
Eight years later and I'm here again,
Nothing's changed, this is English culture.

Kyle Dawney (15)
Borden Grammar School, Sittingbourne

Takeaways

I enter the takeaway, scan the menu above,
A sprightly Indian man with a plastic glove,
I hear the deep fat fryer
Sizzling soothingly,
Smelling our nation's odour.

I order a meal for two; eight pounds fifty,
Across the scorching, greasy barrier
Vinegar stains his apron,
Like brown, salty drip.

The order's gone through, a frantic bustle,
The clanging of pans, the brown bags rustle,
A mass of crispy chips slips and hisses when turned,
The battered medium cod's safely wrapped.

Another order, almost well negotiated,
Great teamwork all around,
The bag is tossed to me, the meal is all right,
As I amble out, leaving into the mild, summer night.

Daniel Oates (15)
Borden Grammar School, Sittingbourne

Match Day

Every Saturday the towns and cities come to life
With the country's passion for football
The cities awake with sound of club songs
The holding of scarves high, with pride
People live and breathe football
Everyone is brought together by football
Every man, woman and child, from every class
come to join in the parade
And are united by this game
Then the entire crowd cram into the colossal stadium
With its imposing towering structures
With a tangy, onion smelling burger
and the stale, sweet smell of beer
The stadium becomes split with colours of blue and red
accentuating tensions between the two opposing sides
When the game starts the stadium lets loose a loud range of noises ranging
from groans to cheers
The fans try to inspire their team to glory
But who will succeed?
Those who win are heroes
Those who lose are the villains
What will your team be?
The losers hold their heads low in astonishment and disbelief
While the winners continue to keep the noise up
hoping for another win next week.

Jonathan Hancock (14)
Borden Grammar School, Sittingbourne

Ignorance

Caribbean man sitting in the street,
Playing his music with no beat,
Caribbean man just sitting there
But does anybody really care?

Guitar in hand, pot by feet,
But will its contents give him food to eat?
I have a feeling, a sense of worry,
But people passing, they just hurry.

I know he'll go cold tonight
And will probably end up in a fight,
A brawl over some space on a stair,
Do you think that's fair?

He needs the money badly
And so he carries on playing, sadly,
But people ignore and just pass,
Thinking his existence is a farce.

And so as I walk to him and his pot,
Money in hand, selfishness forgot,
I feel a sense of self pride,
Before I realise

I am giving him so little and yet it is more,
More than what anyone else will give him,
I feel shame as part of this nation
Who ignore, disrespect and bully.

Oliver McKean (15)
Borden Grammar School, Sittingbourne

The Tree

Sometimes I see them
Two, three or four come past me
Four dressed, going in pairs
Two have a slight haste
Two have a desire to stay on this road
They go with their armour so neat
To battle in the east

They come back, weary from battle
Their armour worn and tired
They talk of the day's conquests
And their hopes of days of nothingness
They go to talk of times ahead
Times past
Going to the west

Sometimes they come on days
In larger or smaller groups
With less ideas of time ahead
Their armour binding them
Only to their colours
They disagree with sun
Going east and west to conquests of their own

They often ask for whom they are fighting
Wondering whether the training will pay them back
Their instructors having been trained
Reasons they cannot fathom to become one
A job in the trades not of labour
A knight would be trained for better
Chances are they'll battle more.

Daniel Catlin (15)
Borden Grammar School, Sittingbourne

Light At The End Of The Tunnel

Nothing can express my deep despair,
I'm so desperate I'd go anywhere.
A place where walls aren't closing in,
Somewhere darkness is not within.
I look up to see a glimpse of light,
All my bright days turn to night.
Lightning bolts surround my home,
But I know I'm not alone.
So many people I don't know,
Actually have no place to go.
No one should live their lives in fear,
We must help each other persevere.
As I sit here looking on,
Staring till the light is gone.
Pray to God our pain will end
And maybe experience peace again.
Scream out for help, but no one hears,
My eyes begin to fill with tears.
But then a hand bursts through the dark,
Sending a blinding, luminous spark.
Picking me up off the floor,
Assuring me there's an end to war.
So all together we must stand,
Binding force, hand in hand.
Helping build a better place,
Bringing hope to the human race.

Jane Abi Farah (15)
Brummana High School, Lebanon

Newly Planted

Wake up and behold the sun,
Watch the skies fight the dark.
That torch is yours to keep lighting,
Put out that flame in your heart.
Recycle that rage within,
Discard the rue, start anew.
Give Earth back its green,
Prosperity comes from inside.
Watch the skies wash down on Africa,
Watch the children in Beirut.
Rise up and renew,
What is gone already flew.
Wake up and come close,
To those 2,000 years apart.
New life could be made true,
Wake up and renew . . .

Stephany Bu Chdid (17)
Brummana High School, Lebanon

Forest Eater

Walking through the sunny field,
A green, gloomy image appears in front of me.
It had brought terror to my heart.
I walked towards it with no knowledge of what lay beyond.
A burned tree had blocked my way, although it was still alive.
Who may have done this to my loving tree?
With a voice that the great Lord could not hear, the tree whispered,
'Indescribable beasts, tearing down our land,
Despite their ferocity you see fear there and terror in their eyes,
Weakness that I have never perceived before.
Destroying all whom they come across.'

Thomas Charles Elkhoury (12)
Brummana High School, Lebanon

A Balance

Earth is not balanced and fair
Rich and poor full of despair
Based on what, at our birth,
We are rich or poor on Earth?
Is it by chance or God's will
Or spots to randomly fill?
Some people are just lucky
Having a lot of money.
Unlike the rest who sleep cold
Hungry, as if no Lord
Darkness fades away the sun
When there's nothing that is done
To fill this gap by the mind
We are all of humankind
Equal, not maid or highness
Zero, not plus or minus
Neutral not acid or base
To make the world a good place
On Earth there is no balance
With it comes a difference.

Frederick Abou Jawdeh (15)
Brummana High School, Lebanon

Poverty

Why does the world always have to be poor?
Why does most of the world always have a bad part?
Is it our destiny that has made it this way
Or nature that has decided to put us in this state?

Why doesn't the world turn around and change the poor to rich?
Or why doesn't the world destiny market change poverty to wealth?

Why must we suffer the pain and sorrow of poverty?
Lord Almighty, help people who are living in poverty
To live in wealth and riches,
So that they can enjoy the fruits of life.

Egbeyemi Eniola (13)
Corona Secondary School, Nigeria

A World Of Difference - Poems From The UK And Around The World

What A War

Oh, what a war!
A war of sorrow and despair,
As women look back to the past.
What a war!

As fathers stay away from home
For so long they forget their own,
As brothers get enlisted
And uncles get killed.
What a war!

As mothers quake at the sight of blood
Like a waterfall.
Gunshots into the night
Like never before.
What a war!

Children too young to understand,
When the dreaded stage of death comes.
Only pictures to remember
The ones once dearly loved.
What a war!

While they all wait for a day,
For the war to stop,
For the sun to shine,
For the stars to rise,
For that heavenly made day
When we shall all say,
The war is over now!

Carmel-Mary Adie (12)
Corona Secondary School, Nigeria

*Young*Writers

War

People killing
people dying
mothers weeping
even afraid
I weep to see
but what I see and feel
I cannot say nor tell
I weep for the innocent
whose blood is spilled

War
Oh war!
Why does everyone not want to listen?
Why do we live in pain and anger?
Oh, my heart aches
and my body shivers!

War!
How bad it is to feel
left in an empty space
left all alone to ponder
if this is not stopped
we will all be gone
let's join hands as one
because we are the one
to stop this thing
we call war!

Joy Ngozi Ojukiou (12)
Corona Secondary School, Nigeria

Pollution

The disruption of our nation
The water, the land and the air
Let us not have to bear
And see no continuation

Pollution
Is it a destructive force
A big observation
A great confusion
When industrial oil
Contaminates our waters

An issue in the brain
We must seek a solution
We must re-channel contaminates
So that
There will better food
It will be very good
Let's endeavour to do.

Malik Anibaba (13)
Corona Secondary School, Nigeria

Rainforest

Our rainforest is a disaster.
People cut down trees all in the name
Of making money, but is that all?
We have more things than that.

We kill our ducks all in the name of food.
Let us leave our ducks and trees alone,
We can make recreational parks,
Most of the things we have are from destructive industries.

When will we open our eyes and see the good,
natural resources that we have?
Should we just sit back, relax and let the white people
Take all our good resources?

We have to do something,
Now, and fast,
We need to wake up
From our deep slumber
And conserve our forests
For a great future
For us and our children.

Rukky Harriman (10)
Corona Secondary School, Nigeria

Poverty

Poverty, poverty
Please go away
We want to be rich
And be successful

Poverty, poverty
Please don't stay
You are stopping people
From arriving at their dreams

Poverty, poverty
I want to achieve my dreams
I want to be rich and great
Please go away.

Sulaiman Maryam (12)
Corona Secondary School, Nigeria

War

With bullets flying all around
And people running helter-skelter,
Chaos is without hinder,
Disrupting all activities with the snap of a finger.

Life-taking and meddling ventures,
Leaving people homeless
And hopeless and despairing
And living without life.

What does it take from us?
Lives that could influence tomorrow,
Infrastructure that could be our fortunes,
Time that could do so many things.

Can't we just live without bad minds?
Can't we just live without impatience?
Can't we just live without anger?
We can, obviously, if we start practising,
Love, compassion, tolerance and encouragement, *now!*

Fashina Tembi (12)
Corona Secondary School, Nigeria

A World Of Difference - Poems From The UK And Around The World

Poverty

What brings sadness?
What brings sorrow?
Something that shows
You are a failure;
Poverty!

What brings lack of food?
What brings lack of money?
Something that shows
You are suffering;
Poverty!

What brings theft?
What brings shame?
A goal that you
Were unable to reach;
Poverty!

What brings death?
What brings sickness?
Your health
You were unable to control;
Poverty!

What brings hunger?
What brings thirst?
Something you were
Unable to carry out first;
Poverty!

Nengi Charles-Ogan (12)
Corona Secondary School, Nigeria

Racism

Black or white
Ivory or ebony
What does it matter? 'Cause
We are the same.

Hispanic or British
African or American
We should stick together, 'Cause
We are the same.

Tall or short
Fat or slim
We should not fight. 'Cause
We are the same.

Colour and nationality
They should not matter
We should share love, 'Cause
We are the same.

Racism must stop
So communism won't flop
Stop I say! 'Cause
We are the same.

People of the world
Come together
We can stop this. 'Cause
We are the same.

Nana Abdulkadir (13)
Corona Secondary School, Nigeria

Racism

Sometimes I seem to wonder
Why blacks are different from white
It is so much to ponder
But racism is not right

Why do we discriminate
If we care less about race
And we stop the criticism
This world can be a better place

We should learn to make peace
We should learn to love
And also live together with ease
We are the same, God created us all, from above.

Adeoye Seyi (11)
Corona Secondary School, Nigeria

Racism

Racism, racism
How bad we blacks suffer
The white treat us like we just don't matter
Why don't we try to make things better?

Why do whites treat us this way?
It's like we don't exist
We are just folded up in one fist
We can try to make peace

Let's try to see each other equally
Made by one person; God
If we work together the world will be better
We can try to respect each other

Racism can be over
Black and white can do it before it's too late
Let's make a treaty of love and peace.

Somto Okoro (11)
Corona Secondary School, Nigeria

War

War, war, when will it stop?
People starving, people dying, all because of war.
If there was something we could do
To save our dying country.
For people to kill themselves
Or even watch people die.
How I wish there was something we could do
So that we can save our dying planet.
War, war, when will it stop?
How dangerous it is.
When will it stop?

Arinze Ochuba (11)
Corona Secondary School, Nigeria

War

Children are weeping
They have lost their parents
Adults are shedding tears
They don't know if they will come back alive.

In this shameful world
Little things build up anger
That degenerates into war
Like hatred sown
And men shut their hearts to pity.

Why don't we change
For the better
Live in peace and be united
For united we stand, divided we fall.

Atinuke Adama (13)
Corona Secondary School, Nigeria

Poverty

Poverty is very bad
In fact it makes you very sad
To know you can't afford a house
As poor as a little church mouse

Poverty makes me sad
In fact it makes me mad
To know you can't afford a car
To go to places both near and far

I don't know how it feels
To be as poor as poor can ever be
Immediately poverty starts
You'll be treated like poor, street rats.

We should build public schools and places
So we won't see poor men as shamed
Poor people should be treated like you and I
Treated kindly and nicely as time passes by.

Akinola Adesomoju (11)
Corona Secondary School, Nigeria

Poverty

Poverty is what makes people not feel free
To have free opportunity in life
Poverty is very bad and happens to anyone
It makes them cry and suffer

So many things can cause poverty
Maybe you did not go to school
Or maybe you are an orphan in the orphanage
Or many other things

We can stop this by providing jobs for the jobless
A manager should employ people
Who are not working
Into their company

Let all learn to be hardworking
Courageous and responsible in the future
Our parents must be up and doing this.

Omotoba Adedapomola Opoolaolywa (10)
Corona Secondary School, Nigeria

Poverty

As the days go by may our nations improve
To make poverty extinct
Make life better for us all
Straighten the path that confuses us
And words cannot say it all
There is evil beneath everything
In our country
Where a few have too much
And many none at all
The gold of this world
Is enough for all people
The reason I am singing the blues
Is that every turn I make
Is a nightmare,
No food, no clothes, no hope
When shall we sing a new song?
When shall there be comfort for all?
When really shall there be gold spread for all?
Let men stop being greedy
Let governments rise to provide basic necessities
Left life be joyous for all.

Christian Daniels (13)
Corona Secondary School, Nigeria

Racism

Racism comes without hesitation,
An act of discrimination,
It is a terrible way of judgement,
Hatred is supplied in abundance.
It is the wrong way of showing difference,
It could be named acuteness.
A word developed called sagacity,
They try to prove supremacy.
Not knowing that we are all equal,
All their cautions are feeble.
A high amount of wisdom is needed,
Together this problem can be resolved and treated.

Shodipo Bola (14)
Corona Secondary School, Nigeria

Pollution

Pollution you need a solution
Although it seems impossible
Pollution must not be beyond bounds
So we must stand our ground

Let's find a way to stop pollution
Even though the solution is not in sight
But we will not give up our reclamation
So we must save our generation
And stand as one nation

Now we have a goal
And that goal is to stop pollution
Now we have to fulfil our role
And we must achieve that goal
And that goal is to stop pollution
Everyone must speak to their neighbours
God will not come from Heaven
We must control ourselves
Out our rubbish in the garbage bin and not on the streets.

Fafaa Meheux (12)
Corona Secondary School, Nigeria

Litter

Drop your litter into the dustbin,
Not on the floor
And that will make your dirty litter
Not touch your nice clean floor.

For all around us there are germs
And the litter doesn't make it better,
It further destroys your environment,
But cleanliness could make it better.

So, dear friends, please do not drop your litter around,
Use the litter bin,
Then our environment could be better,
Life would be healthy and enjoyable.

Popoola Foalshade (12)
Corona Secondary School, Nigeria

Replenishing The Earth

When shall we realise
That this world is not meant to be destabilised?
In so many ways we have reorganised
What our Creator has improvised
When shall we realise
That not all around is music?
Some of the sound we hear
Is made from the chainsaws
Cutting down what is left of the rainforests
When shall we understand
That by thinking of ourselves alone
And exploiting for our own gain
We have abused the world around us?
How shall we correct this wrong
Of lifelong consequences?
The air, filled up with foul stench from pollution
The waters, filled up with sediments and debris
Even the lands are dried up
As a result of various human activities
How shall we cleanse our land
Of the dirt littered everywhere?
The creatures and plants are being destroyed every day
We need the knowledge to replenish and restore them
Our natural resources are lost because of greed and corruption
So many people are dying of numerous diseases all the time
We need a solution to this problem
A way out of the mess we have created for ourselves
We need the power and the wisdom
To restore our world
And make humanity a better place for all.

EbunOluwe Oduntan (13)
Corona Secondary School, Nigeria

War

People killing people
People dying
Children missing
Parents crying

What would the world be without war?
Without people risking their lives
Just for other people to be saved?
It would be a peaceful world

Ambush lies everywhere
Sometimes just for the fun of it
Sometimes just over an argument
Nothing more

Pow! Pow! Pow!
Goes the gunshots
And then the bombs
Could it get any worse?

After all we did
Trying to make the world a better place
But did it work out
No it didn't

In the end, what do you see?
Humans littering everywhere you go
Who would pick the dead up?
No one, no one, no one.

Salau Oluwatosin (12)
Corona Secondary School, Nigeria

Our World

People are killing,
People are dying,
Children on the streets are crying.
There are wars, there are foes
They cause trauma and woes.

Our world is dying
Because we wouldn't hear its crying.
Our trees being cut down,
Our animals being killed
And its effect on us is more than a frown.

People litter the roads,
Because the floods wash them away.
Our land is polluted
In every single way.

Some 'whites' hate 'blacks'
And 'blacks' hate 'whites'
And we all know that it's not right.
Some people have nowhere to live,
That's why it's good for us to give.

We children are rotten
Our slangs from where are gotten?
And our ways get worse
Making our parents remorse.

We can change this world,
We can live in eternal bliss,
If we trust in God
If only we could love one another
And do a little good to someone.

I know we can do it
But only if
We aspire to acquire
The desire we admire.

And there would be nothing more,
Than peace without war.

Damilola Sotuminu (11)
Corona Secondary School, Nigeria

The Good-natured Citizens

Foul smelling air filled the atmosphere
Like that of decayed materials
The ground groaned mournfully
As dirt swept it passionately

Everyone passed by dumpsters
Most seemed not to care
Wind raised up particles
Which made breathing almost impossible

The good-natured citizens
Thought to change the situation
By clearing all dumpsters
And stopping any interference

Things worked out according to plan
And the air was clear again
Now we can breathe well once again
Thanks to the good-natured citizens.

Dairo Praise (15)
Demonstration Secondary School, Nigeria

Poverty

The enemy of men,
Oh! thou art so mean,
You have come to destroy,
Without any pity on anyone,
Oh! poverty, why art thou so wicked?

You have caused the death of so many souls,
You alone have made men go insane,
You have made many weep,
You have made many downcast,
Oh! poverty, why art thou so wicked?

You have caused the discrimination of many,
Making men look down on those who are affected by you,
You have made many lose hope in this world,
Oh! poverty, why art thou so wicked?

You have made many homeless,
Due to wars and earthquake,
Bringing down the homes of many,
Leaving them homeless,
Without them having anything to rebuild their homes,
Oh! poverty, why art thou so wicked?

Ehinlaiye Mercy Oiza (16)
Demonstration Secondary School, Nigeria

The Wildlife

The amazing works of nature
Have given to us great creatures of beauty,
Creatures both fierce, wild and tame.
They were given to us as additives and supplements,
To beautify our surroundings
And add to the fascinating world of wildlife.

But what has become of this beautiful scenario?
It has been reduced to something of no importance,
All because of Man's daily activities.
Oil spillage, bush burning have driven our animals away.
The world of industrialisation has helped in effacing our animals,
All in the form of industrial waste.

Man's greed and lust for money
Has triggered the hunting of beautiful animals.
Animals like the dodo bird amongst others,
Have long been obliterated for reasons unexplainable.
The fear of animal extinction has now reached the hearts of many,
The old generation are in fear for their successors.

What shall their knowledge of animals be?
Will they just see them in books and not for real?
Some beliefs talk of new paradise,
Where people can see all kinds of animals,
Others believe in the magic of science
To bring back our extinct beasts,
Which may be an illusion!

Igonoh Joy Abodiya (17)
Demonstration Secondary School, Nigeria

Transport

The big, white, flying beast hovers in the sky,
The roaring sound of the engines running through my ears,
Who knew these machines could kill?
Animals, water, air and sky,
Dying, dying.
The Earth is dead,
We are murderers,
But we also give life,
We are stewards of the Earth,
We control the future,
We created the past,
Recycle, use a bicycle
And together we will be creators.

Manasseh Dalton-Brown (13)
Finchley Catholic High School, Finchley

Pollution - That Hand

That hand is so vital,
It can damage the ball,
That one little drop
Can destroy us all.
That one little thing
Can be so small.
However, the pollution
Still grows tall!

Guiliano Cinotti (13)
Finchley Catholic High School, Finchley

Ice Caps

The ice caps are melting
Nobody cares
Nobody trying to stop it
The world is dying
We are dying
People are trying
But people are failing
We are trying to stop it
People are giving ideas
But they are not going to happen.

Michael Gallagher (13)
Finchley Catholic High School, Finchley

Goodbye Rainforest

The rainforests are leaving,
All will go,
No animals will survive
The bulldozer's blows.
Their homes all gone,
The family mostly dead,
But it's all on our head.
We're the ones who did this,
We cannot hide,
Just think,
Do we need paper
to
    survive?

Christopher McCarthy (13)
Finchley Catholic High School, Finchley

The Light And Dark Of Earth

The yellow cries of the scorching sun,
heats up billions, yet it is one.
Up above the world so high,
like the oven of the sky.
Down through holes above the Earth,
newborn babies failed at birth.
Shadow, shadow of the night,
contrasts the sun's blinding light.
Clinging blackness chokes and holds,
to the life of young and old.
Death to humans its single goal,
heart is black with deadly soul.

David Odum (13)
Finchley Catholic High School, Finchley

Our World

The layer is broken and the rays are flying,
People are crying words of wisdom.
Factories are coughing dark black smoke,
People are being ignorant, dropping litter.
Animals are dying, suffering and crying;
You can stop this; be the one
Who stops the crying and the warming up.
Help us please and alter the future,
This is it, it's
Our world.

Simon Saldanha (13)
Finchley Catholic High School, Finchley

The Bicycle

I'm sitting in a car, oh what a sight!
Fumes coming out everywhere into the light.
The sun is glaring down with a heat unbearable,
Why can't everyone use a bicycle?

I see people passing down riding on bikes,
Why can't I be doing that? Why not me?
But now the sun's glaring down, looking at me,
I look up at the sky, I can hardly see anything,
Because there are fumes in the sky that are covering everything.

I don't know what to do, because I'm not very sure,
Maybe I should ride a bicycle more.

Aaron Rebak (13)
Finchley Catholic High School, Finchley

Bin

Please rubbish, go in the bins
When you look around you see our rubbish building up.
We think our world is some big bin.

Litter, it makes us very bitter
To see our world full of litter.
Please litter, go to the bin where you belong.

People dropping Coke bottles, plastic bottles and glass,
Making our world a messy place.
Please rubbish, go in the bin and don't come again.

Rubbish, rubbish, please go away,
Let us have a happy day.

Stephen Mead (13)
Finchley Catholic High School, Finchley

Greenhouse

Greenhouse lying in the garden,
Feeling yourself warm up.
Watching animals and plants grow up inside you,
Then suddenly, gas breaks out.
Animals start to choke, plants start to die,
Fruits start to rot, screaming for mercy.

But we ignore these calls,
Making animals and plants suffer,
This is our wake up call!

Massimo Perdoni (13)
Finchley Catholic High School, Finchley

Rainforest

Through the thick cloudy mist,
Lies a secret world to discover.
Where tigers hunt, monkeys climb,
Rabbits hide, birds communicate.
The rain falls, *pitte- patter, pitter-patter.*
Loud, rare, special, secret, no more!
The noise is pierced by a loud treacherous death;
A scream, a choke, a bullet.
The forest is no more!

Marios Leonidou (13)
Finchley Catholic High School, Finchley

Being Homeless

The rough, tired soul
As he has no home
All by himself, alone.

People walk by and throw 10p
When what he needs is a home
And family.

The freezing air
As cold as ice
The drunken men walk by
And give him a fright.

The hunger gets greater
The box as a bed
He has no home
Might as well be dead.

Help the poor
Open a centre
To help the poor
And make them better.

Sam Vanellis (13)
Finchley Catholic High School, Finchley

Stop Gun And Knife Crime

Not a day goes by
Without somebody getting shot or stabbed

Why put their friends through hell?
They're dreading if they hear a bell

Policemen standing outside
Saying, 'Sorry to inform you, your son has died.'

Parents shouldn't worry
And kids shouldn't need to hurry

Playing on the street has become a risk;
Police searching for weapons while they frisk

So please put guns and knives down
Don't make another mother frown.

Dominic Zohreh (13)
Finchley Catholic High School, Finchley

World Today

Rainforest trees being cut down
Seeing wars doesn't even make us frown
More homeless people dying
And we aren't even trying

We drop litter on our streets
Racism from those we meet
Leaving our TVs on at night
Yet climate change gives us a fright?

Connor Geraghty (13)
Finchley Catholic High School, Finchley

Recycle

R ainforests being cut down
E xtinction of animals
C onflicts turning to wars
Y obs polluting little towns
C limate change
L itter
E viction from homes due to waste of resources.

Matthew Fernandez (13)
Finchley Catholic High School, Finchley

Planet Earth

S cience says we're wasting away
A nd both Poles are melting
V ery soon we'll be unde water
E xtinct, the animals are going

U ganda is suffering
S o is Ethiopia.

Cameron Wallis (13)
Finchley Catholic High School, Finchley

Dirty Waste

Poverty, it's quite big in the streets,
All due to litter, e.g. chewing gum underneath your seat.
The homeless man now lives in the gutter,
Praying for some bread and a little bit of butter.

We waste a lot, throw out too much litter,
To be in poverty life can be quite bitter.
Dreaming about when you'll get a three course meal,
Living in the cold winter night, how does it feel?

So stop throwing out your garbage,
Keep it away,
Homeless preaching,
Just to see another day.

Edem Delor (13)
Finchley Catholic High School, Finchley

War

People scream as bullets fly around
But they're not the only ones screaming

Animals' homes are being destroyed by fire
Their children lie still in rivers flowing with Earth's blood

The Earth has holes as deep as slash wounds
And people's bodies lie in them

Why are we here in this bloodshed?
Why not make peace for our children's sake?

Daniel Carey (13)
Finchley Catholic High School, Finchley

Why Can't We?

Cars, factories, electrical appliances, planes,
It all seems insane.
The way we use them is mad.
It makes the world ever so sad.
If we turn the killers on,
Using appliances won't be fun.
Soon they will take, we won't be able to hide.
The world will be destroyed from the inside out.
With all the pain, it won't be able to shout.
The time has come for this giant man
To look deep down, take control and do what we can.
Together we are a body, a soul, we are one.
Why break that by leaving the TV on?

Kaif Agbaje (13)
Finchley Catholic High School, Finchley

No Time To Waste

So here we are
But now we've gone too far.
Work we have to do,
But they don't have a clue.

The chainsaw sizzles
And laughs at the falling trees.
It demands more.

The animal population goes down,
Yet the men do not frown.
The dams struggle to keep the water out
And the people are begging for a drought.

But it's still not too late
For people to change their actions.
But we must hurry,
As there is not much time the Earth can wait!

Michele D'Alessio (13)
Finchley Catholic High School, Finchley

Can You Stop It?

Unfatigued it spreads like wildfire,
Killing all in its path.
Who can stop it?

Young, old, male ,female,
No one is safe.
Who can stop it?

On and on it goes
With its dance so merry,
With its slow beat of death and destruction.
A result of our own ignorance.

Do what you can.
There is nowhere to hide.
You can slow it down,
But
Can you stop it?

Geofrey Banzi (13)
Finchley Catholic High School, Finchley

Raining, Raining

The bigger they are, the harder they fall
If a tree falls and nobody is around, does it make a sound?
The land is being crushed, pulverised by the wooden ocean
Their legs amputated by the twisting of the saw

Children on branches screaming as they swim through the blinding air
Homes being torn apart by men's intentions
'Timber,' the word that strikes them with fear
Crash! The sound of the impact as she cries

The Earth's soil being scraped through cruelty, not strength
Green being turned to gold by the minute
The brown ocean lies there, still as a rock
Dead, life gone in hours, bye-bye rainforest.

Arthur Bayele (13)
Finchley Catholic High School, Finchley

Recycling

R each for the little black bin
E ach can could run a computer for 20 minutes
C an you save your country?
Y ou can do it
C an you do your part?
L earn to recycle
I n Africa, children die every day
N inety percent of children starve
G o get some cans to recycle.

Alex Alfano (13)
Finchley Catholic High School, Finchley

For The Future

We should be green
Instead of being mean
To our wonderful planet
Just turn off your TV
There's many ways to save the trees
Just everyone at least try
Then your children can see how we lived
You should want that too, one way is to reuse.

Jay John Flaherty (13)
Finchley Catholic High School, Finchley

Fishes

It was a very popular place
Where everyone went
It's a place to race
Where fishes pace

The water is too dirty
So the fishes are gone
The water is becoming empty
No fishes are coming along

There's only one way for them
We need to help them
By saving the world again
Like more recycling and saving energy.

Stephen Murphy (13)
Finchley Catholic High School, Finchley

The Sun

The sun is bright
Generating light
Sometimes damaging your sight
It may melt you but it won't bite

The sun is hot
Like a boiling pot
Making ice flaming hot
Can it be cold? Obviously not!

The sun goes down
Without a frown
The sun has gone down
It's our turn now.

James Davin (13)
Finchley Catholic High School, Finchley

Recycling

The Earth is like a great big sphere,
It's an open wound for garbage to appear,
So we should all start recycling
To make the world a better place.

When you walk down the street
There's litter on the floor,
If this keeps on the Earth could become poor,
So people, make the world a better place,
Recycle!

Ryan O'Halloran (13)
Finchley Catholic High School, Finchley

A World Of Difference - Poems From The UK And Around The World

How Would You Feel?

How would you feel
If you couldn't breathe
In your home because of pollution?
How would you feel?

How would you feel
If you went to a park
On a summer's evening
And there was rubbish everywhere?
How would you feel?

How would you feel
If an animal was being strangled to death
Because of the rubbish you left?
How would you feel?

The world is changing,
I want to wake up.
The world is changing,
I want to wake up.

Chris O'Toole (13)
Finchley Catholic High School, Finchley

Protectors Of The Earth

Chocolate and sweet wrappers in the streets
There's rubbish, waste here and there
Do we not care?
We are people
Protectors of the Earth
It is simple
Don't drop litter on the turf!

Killing animals
Killing bears
Thinking of their long white hair
Cutting down trees
Killing bees
While the bees say, 'Please!'

Sean Griffin (13)
Finchley Catholic High School, Finchley

Pollution

There is pollution everywhere
The Earth cries painful tears
That burn the trees bare

The ice melting
The weather is changing
Places are flooding

There is gas in the air
That is killing the Earth
We need to stop using cars.

Duval Omo (13)
Finchley Catholic High School, Finchley

War And Racism

Why war?
Why not peace?
War was created for beating up others to gain land.
But some wars are over racism.
Like the killing of millions of Jews in World War II.

Why racism?
Why not peace?
Why was racism created?
What's the point of racism?
We are all the same, whatever we look like.
We should be treated the same.
But that's how life goes.

What's worse, racism or war?
I say racism.
Well, wars are created by debates
And racism is a big debate.

Felipe Dinis (13)
Finchley Catholic High School, Finchley

The Mean War

The war, the mean war
Once you're shot, you fall
But down in the trench
Is where it gets all tense
You can't take any more

When the general shouts
The fire goes out
The spirits go low
And you just say no
To all the fighting
It's just so frightening

I wish I were more bright
To know there is no light
At the end of this fight
But now I can see my home
I've changed my tone
I'm ready to go home.

Christopher Kanor (13)
Finchley Catholic High School, Finchley

A Complaint To The Council

Green, green
Why isn't everything
So green
Anymore?
People always cutting down trees
It's not needed even though it can be done with care

Animals, animals
Why aren't there many animals
Anymore?
People cutting their skin
For our luxuries
But must you use things to make money?

Dirty, dirty
Why is the world so dirty
All the time?
Folks always littering in public places
Why is it so hard to
Keep it clean
Anymore?
You do it in your own home
Don't you?

None of these things are right
I don't want to have to fight about this
But it isn't right
So why do it?

Sope Soetan (13)
Finchley Catholic High School, Finchley

Recycling

I saw some litter on the floor,
We can't live like this anymore.
We are scarring our world and soon we'll pay,
For the huge pile of litter, increasing each day.

We'll kill our world beyond repair,
The animals we love will not be there.
So I put the litter in the recycling bin,
To leave it there would be an unforgivable sin.

Stefano Silva (13)
Finchley Catholic High School, Finchley

Pollution

P ut your rubbish in the bin
O ur lifestyle has been affected by pollution
L itter has affected us and animals
L ove for our homes
U nderstand you are the ones who have caused this
T ry and be more eco-friendly
I n a few years this world will be destroyed
O n this subject, just be good for yourself and others
N o more pollution.

Jake Cloney (13)
Finchley Catholic High School, Finchley

I Am A Snowy White Polar Bear

I am a snowy white polar bear
All alone, no one to care
As the evil sun shines down on me
That very sun that killed my family
Destroyed my home
The ice melts,
My land fades away,
Smaller and smaller
Till no more
I do fear I will disappear
Where do I go from here?

Stefano Kempster (13)
Finchley Catholic High School, Finchley

The Planet's Changing

G reen is the colour of grass.
R ising pollution is going to turn the grass grey.
E nvironment, we need to act before it's too late.
E veryone needs your help to stop the rise in pollution.
N ow is the time to act!

Oliver Collins (13)
Finchley Catholic High School, Finchley

How Green Changes

Green, green, green, the world is full of green
But not for long, pollution, war, cars, factories,
Things that we use daily, all destroying green.

We all love green, it is mostly in gardens,
It's colourful, it makes us happy.

But why, why, why are we, *yes us,* destroying it?

We can help it, we can recycle,
Don't take the car, take public transport,
What causes all of this?
What is the cause of pollution?
Us!

Mark Gibbs (13)
Finchley Catholic High School, Finchley

Pollution

The Earth is our community,
We have to look after it together,
And we are doing the complete opposite
We have to stop pollution, now!
We have to take action now, before it's too late,
We have to save the Earth,
To do this we have to recycle and not pollute.

It is not too late to save the Earth,
But there is one condition,
We will have to do it together.

Antonio Evangelista (13)
Finchley Catholic High School, Finchley

Four Wheel Symphony

Every corner and every gap
They hold their ground or sneak about
The metal machines race around,
Monsters of the road.

No time to run or hide,
There is nowhere to go,
The machines are everywhere you look,
Guzzling petrol like whales eat krill.

Their mission is to burn the Earth,
Their gas killing our protective shield,
But they should know pollution is not the way,
As the sun shows no mercy.

Michael De Luca (13)
Finchley Catholic High School, Finchley

The World

In this world there is so much war,
People coming to tell you bad news at the door.
Loads of people die
And you have to say goodbye.
This is the world.

This world has pollution, buses and cars,
You just wish it was all on Mars.
Big polluting buses in red,
Like a bad dream in your head.
This is the world.

This world makes me so sad,
It also makes me very mad!
People don't try to keep it clean,
Because they are lazy and mean.
Is this the world?

Louis Comerford (13)
Finchley Catholic High School, Finchley

Untitled

Message in a bottle
Floating in the sea
Should have been recycled
Glass for you and me.

Paper by the roadside
Scrunched up in a ball
Should have been recycled
Paper for you and me.

Tin can in the gutter
Rusty as can be
Should have been recycled
Metal for you and me.

Cardboard in the garbage
Soaked and stained with food
Should have been recycled
Cardboard for you and me.

T-shirt in the river
Torn up and ripped throughout
Should have been recycled
Clothes for you and me.

Plastic milk bottle
Littering the grass
Should have been recycled
Plastic for you and me.

This paper for the poem
Recycled in a way
Turn over and you'll see
Recycling for you and me.

Jonathan Warren (12)
Hardenhuish School, Chippenham

Recycle

We all want to keep our world clean
Unlike you I'm not mean.
While others are
Recycling a car,
You could just recycle your jeans.

We don't want to hurt the ozone layer,
You might be a good football player.
Help the Earth,
On your birth,
And then you might meet the mayor.

You don't want to get any fatter,
So recycle all your clatter,
If you just would,
Give all your wood,
Don't worry, yours will still make the matter.

When you drink a bottle of water,
It could have been your daughter,
Put it in the box,
Not for the fox,
It won't make the world's life shorter.

Charlie Kingsley (12)
Hardenhuish School, Chippenham

Fossil Fuels

Fossil fuels float in the air,
It leaves the globe in great despair,
Reduce your carbon footprint now,
And stop the ozone burning, somehow!

Reduce, reuse, recycle now
And stop the trees being cut down.

Sam Wiggins (12)
Hardenhuish School, Chippenham

The Disgraceful Environment

Look out the window,
What do you see?
A pile of litter and just one tree.

We could help this world,
And make it a happy planet.

Recycling will make the world merry and bright
And stopping pollution will give animals delight.
Trees keep us alive, so why cut them down?
No trees mean no smiles, just a frown.

Crime and vandalism make people sad,
Carrying a weapon is stupid and bad!
If we want to change the world where we live,
Our message should be don't take, *give!*

Tom Jones (11)
Hardenhuish School, Chippenham

Litter

Litter, litter on the floor,
Don't drop litter anymore,
Clear our streets that are full of trash,
Get out of your chair! It's time to dash.

Litter, litter on the streets,
Old newspapers,
Wrappers from sweets,
Let's clean up that awful mess,
From public fields
To trapped crisps in wire mesh.

Put your litter in the bin,
Clear up this awful sin,
Make our Earth feel much better,
Now there's no more litter on the floor.

Henry Trutch (12)
Hardenhuish School, Chippenham

Green Giant

(This poem is all about a green giant that looked after our world in the past but then turned evil and is now ruining the world. Just like what is happening in our world today! But with people being the giants!)

Green Giant ruled the universe,
Green Giant ruled the sea.
I looked out of my window,
Green Giant I could see.

Shutting off electricity stations,
Switching off house lights,
He very much enjoyed his job,
Much to his delight!

His spell made tree cutters fall to sleep,
And smashed every printer up,
Because they wasted so much paper,
Trees just couldn't keep up!

One day he then turned evil,
Disobeying the rules of his job,
This made the whole wide world completely,
All turn into slobs!

Now today we're awful,
TV is our thing,
Gas is rising into the air,
No one really seems to care 'bout everything disappearing.

We should change,
Change our ways,
Back to them,
Good old days!

Bring back Mr Big Green Giant,
So we can succeed in making our world a better place,
To make our world triumphant!

Charlotte Myers (12)
Hardenhuish School, Chippenham

The Environment

Don't cut down trees,
Or pollute the seas.
If you're not going far,
Don't get in your car.
Cycling is the way to go,
To keep your carbon footprint low.
Turn off the lights, unplug the TV,
Saving the planet is up to you and me.
Bottles, paper, cans and tins,
Put them in your recycling bins.
Renewable energy will last forever
If we stay smart and keep it clever.
Use solar panels and wind turbines,
Instead of digging more coal mines.
Pollution of this fantastic Earth
Has been happening since the day of our birth.
Please don't let it carry on,
It's our children who'll suffer when it's gone.

Callum Harnden (11)
Hardenhuish School, Chippenham

Help Our World

The world truly is a really great place,
But in a way it's always a disgrace.
There's trash on the floor, and in the air,
That's only because most don't care.
A hole in the ozone needs our attention,
So to all our friends we must mention.
The world needs help as you can see,
I don't care, just let me be.
The end of the world is coming soon,
As no one is helping it'll be after the moon.

Thomas Cavaciuti (12)
Hardenhuish School, Chippenham

Help Us!

Do you want to see your planet die of junk,
The muck, the rubbish and all that stuff?

Do you want to see your planet go wrong in so many ways,
Rain in the summer and heat on a winter's day?

There's a few things that you can help us do,
Such as reduce, reuse and recycle

So help us make a greener day for all
The generations that come our way.

Ryan Cuss (11)
Hardenhuish School, Chippenham

The Dying Planet

Planet Earth is dying.

Its lakes and rivers drying,
Its creatures perishing,
Its forests falling,
Its ozone burning,
Its countryside disappearing.

Its people destroying,
Their wars scaring,
Their vehicles poisoning,
Their numbers growing,
Their lifetime increasing,

Their existence shortening,

Planet Earth is dying.

Stop the wars,
Change the vehicles,
Save the creatures,
Help the ozone,
Protect the countryside,
Grow new forests,
Fill the lakes and rivers,
Recycle waste,
Reuse items.

Save Planet Earth!

Tom Bunce (12)
Hardenhuish School, Chippenham

Untitled

Each branch on a tree,
I can see,
Children playing and running free.

Don't cut down the big green tower,
Why don't you let it show its power,
Let it give air if you care.

Each blade of grass,
Each honey tree,
Keep on recycling,
So my mum told me.

Alana Brokenshire
Hardenhuish School, Chippenham

Changes

Plant a tree
And watch it grow,
Clean the rivers,
To help them flow.

Check the label,
Check it twice,
Make sure it's free-range,
Very nice!

The grass is green
And so are you,
So pick up some rubbish
And recycle it too.

Lily Brett (12)
Hardenhuish School, Chippenham

Trees And Rainforests

Trunks are brown,
Leaves are green,
Trees are actually evergreen.

Deforestation,
A fancy name for cutting down trees,
Causes lots of animals to flee.

Sunny hot months,
Trees transpire heat,
Causing us not to look like sizzled meat!

Monsoon season opens like the mouth of a river,
Under the evergreens is shelter from storms,
Monsoons close like a clutch of a claw.

Non evergreens die,
After time goes by
And the tree cycle starts all over again!

Trunks are grey,
Leaves are dead,
This comes as quickly as a bang on your head!

Alex Bartlett (11)
Hardenhuish School, Chippenham

World At War

The way to end a mighty war,
Is to end it with a mighty roar,
We planned for a mighty boom,
That would send them all off to the moon.

As we planned for the move,
We were ambushed out of the blue,
As I heard the bullets go past,
I wished it would end really fast.

Then I stood looking to the sky,
I heard the boom in front of my eyes,
My ears popped as I felt the shock,
I hit the floor and a rock.

As I felt the blood on my hand,
I think I needed a helping hand,
I felt the pain strike my neck,
Then I felt like a nervous wreck.

As I knew the pain would end,
I realised my life had come to an end.

Louie Baker (13)
Hardenhuish School, Chippenham

Animals

Animals are our friends,
But little do we know,
How we are killing them,
Destroying their homeland.

Cutting down all the trees,
Is killing all the birds,
Cutting down all the trees,
Is killing all the bees.

Ruining habitats,
The coral reef, a pond,
The ice caps, your back garden,
The rainforest, it's gone.

It's going, it's going,
It's going, it's going,
It's going, it's going,
It's going, it's gone.

Amy Hamilton (13)
Hardenhuish School, Chippenham

The Future

What does the future hold for us?
Smog-filled skies and poisonous cars,
And broken land with useless dust
And nature's beauty behind bars.

Can I ever show my children,
If they ever come my way,
The beauty of the sunset,
At the ending of the day?

Can I walk into a forest
And surround myself with trees,
Yet know that it will remain,
For me to visit as I please?

I know that I can today,
Do all the things I've said,
But when today is yesterday,
Will all these things be dead?

This problem is enormous,
As we gradually take heed,
So we must fix it quickly,
Using words and thoughts and deeds.

Abigail Willcox (12)
Hardenhuish School, Chippenham

A World Of Difference -Poems From The UK And Around The World

The Ballad Of The Blue Whale

Magnificent monarch of the sea,
Gentle giant beneath the waves,
Riding the waters majestically,
In search of the lonely graves.

Listening for the longed for song,
That would tell him he was not alone,
Needing desperately to belong,
To ease his lonely heart's groan.

Distant memories of the past,
Echo dimly through his mind,
Swimming freely, strong and fast,
Where are the others? Is he the last?

Once a member of the crowd,
Roaming through their aquatic kingdom,
United in strength, unafraid and proud,
How can they have lost their freedom?

Finally discovered, the other whales,
In the darkest depths, a glimmer of white shows.
Hoping against hope, yet his courage fails,
For deep inside he knows.

The sea has been turning steadily black,
Surrounded by oil, he starts to choke,
What is this insane attack?
The sea is filled with vicious smoke.

Magnificent monarch of the sea,
Struggling to breathe beneath the waves.
Aching body, mind and heart weary,
Sinking to join the other graves.

Simon Munday (12)
Hardenhuish School, Chippenham

Untitled

Labour, Lib Dem, Conservative
We have them all,
The Green Party however,
At the back of the hall.

The ozone layer,
The ever growing hole,
The same as a human,
That has no soul.

From when I was little,
I was always aware,
The damage people cause,
Without any care.

But now things are bad,
Worse than ever before,
CO_2, climate change,
Carbon emissions and more.

The environment is changing,
And now in our hands,
To change the future of the Earth,
By recycling things like cans.

Recycle, reuse, reduce,
Just some of the things you can do,
To save this, our ill planet,
Not just for me, but for you.

Emily Terrell
Hardenhuish School, Chippenham

Panda

Here is a panda sitting on the floor,
Eating bamboo, he doesn't care about the boar,
But when a hunter comes in with a double-barrelled gun,
All the panda wants to do is run.

Bang, bang, bang bullets flying past his head,
Soon the panda will be very much dead.
He keeps on running further into the wood,
Trying to stay away from the man who stood.

Bang, bang, again, poor, poor panda,
Gone for evermore onto the granda,
The panda is gone forever more,
Soon will they all - for evermore!

Jack Swan
Hardenhuish School, Chippenham

Extinction

Extinction, extinction, extinction,
What a horrible thing it is,
It is when an animal is no more,
Now, just think about this.

Endangered is another word,
Where an animal is almost wiped out,
Africa is full of endangered species,
Now, how did that come about?

It's because of us humans,
We hunt animals for their meat,
Or maybe for their skin, or ivory,
For us to stop killing animals would be, oh so sweet!

Humans need to stop murdering,
Animals such as the elephant,
We're making other horrors stop,
But extinction and endangerment need also to be relevant!

Some animals are already extinct,
Such as the dinosaur and the dodo,
This awful hunting business,
Seems horribly popular at the mo!

Extinction, extinction, extinction,
Will soon become the fate of the tiger and the bear,
It's our job to stop it happening, but we're not doing our duty,
Now isn't that so unfair . . . unfair . . . unfair!

Kayleigh Ward (13)
Hardenhuish School, Chippenham

Rubbish

We see so many people,
Tomorrow or today,
Who actually refuse,
To simply throw their rubbish away.

Is it too much hassle,
Or too much pain,
To keep our once pretty streets,
Looking reasonably sane?

Is it too much aggravation,
To walk to the nearest bin,
To put your hand above,
And just drop it in?

So the next time you're thinking,
Of carelessly littering,
Think of the sick world,
And do the right thing.

Kara Buffrey (14)
Hardenhuish School, Chippenham

Environmental Ballad

There are many things that you can do,
To cure this environmental flu,
The ozone layer has a massive hole,
It's lucky for us that it's by a Pole.

If you just use your car less,
Then it's definitely for the best,
It puts fewer gases in the air,
That harms our precious ozone layer.

Recycling things can help Earth too,
It's an amazing thing you can easily do,
If you recycle the newspaper that you seek,
It can become a new one in just a week.

When you leave a room next time,
Turn the light off and don't whine,
Don't leave your TV on standby,
It uses too much electricity.

Now you know what you should do,
So get on and help cure Earth's flu.

Ben Watts-Jones (13)
Hardenhuish School, Chippenham

A World Of Difference -Poems From The UK And Around The World

Homeless Cats

My body is aching and filled with pain,
I crawl and jump, as I run in the rain,
It's such a dangerous world outside for cats,
With fast cars, dogs and poisonous rats.

All those who go on holiday and leave us by ourselves,
All those who think us cats can magically feed themselves,
In the house, my jumpers, laid out on my favourite chair,
But what's the use of comfort, if your owner isn't there?

I'm so tired and hungry and cold,
As once my friend foretold;
'I'd sleep in the bushes,
With scratching branches,

I'd run in the streets just looking for scraps,
It's horrible out there, just like a death trap.'
Will that be me caught in a storm?
How about somewhere safe and warm?

I'm unwanted now, no one cares,
So get rid of these nightmares,
Take them away,
I don't want to stay.

Hide in a bush without any food,
With only sadness and a sleepy mood,
Soon I will die,
For death's not a lie.

We'll starve to death,
Without a breath,
Not even on a cosy mat,
But that's the life for us homeless cats.

Alice Massingham
Hardenhuish School, Chippenham

Bike

Too many people are using a car,
It's killing our world, making it sick,
Ride on a horse, you could go just as far,
Just jump on and give it a kick.

It's good for the world but not for the horse,
But what else could we use? Maybe a bus,
Or a train, I know, of course,
I'll use a bike, that's no fuss.

I can pedal all day in the fresh air,
I'll be quite free roaming the Earth,
There will be no cost, just the wind in my hair,
I can ride and not worry what it's worth.

Our world needs help, please look after it,
It wants to get better, it needs you,
Don't use your car if you can help it,
Just think about what you should and shouldn't do.

Ellen Gaunt (13)
Hardenhuish School, Chippenham

The Environment

We're so lucky to have this Earth,
It's such a beautiful place,
So why do we have to ruin it,
Us: the human race?

We churn the Earth and use ours cars,
We don't seem to care,
The world we know will soon be gone,
Generations please beware.

Us selfish lot, few are green,
We need to recycle more,
Save our water and our glass,
Pick litter off the floor.

If we do this we'll only gain,
It's definitely not wrong,
Our future grandchildren will have this Earth,
But certainly not for long.

So save that last piece of paper,
Don't throw that final pot,
And remember to cut your emissions,
Together we can save the lot.

Catherine Cox-Field (13)
Hardenhuish School, Chippenham

Rainforest

The rainforest is where the animals live,
And a home to many tribes,
Even though it is just a word,
To young adults like you and me.

Insects are climbing up the vine,
The sun is streaming down,
A rainforest is my entire life,
It means the world to me.

This rainforest used to blanket Brazil,
But now it shrinks and tightens,
Our green will trap the monkeys and spiders,
Frogs and birds, you and me.

Rosina Brown (12)
Inveralmond Community High School, Livingston

War

Smoke curls from the war zone,
The constant cackle of automatic fire,
Blood running like rivers.

Thundering behemoth,
Bringing death to us all,
Destroyers of worlds.

Screams of children,
Families slaughtered,
People think this is fun.

David Henderson (14)
Inveralmond Community High School, Livingston

Cyclone

C yclone hits, people look on in horror,
Y oung children scream violently for their families,
C rowds of people gather at their windows,
L ooking helpless and vulnerable, they sit in fear,
O ver the thick clouds, terror appears,
N ever looking back, the people run for their lives like terrified prey,
E scape the only concern of the terror approaching.

Lois Moncrieff (14)
Inveralmond Community High School, Livingston

Summer Haiku

Summertime is here,
Shades, sunbathing and late nights,
Sunset, beautiful.

Ashley Middlemass (14)
Inveralmond Community High School, Livingston

Outside The Four Walls

Glare of students and teachers.
Sun is artificial through dirty windows.
Sky is shut out by unforgiving walls.
That pile of books only holds suffocating work.
Birds give no respect for the school;
It's just a façade.
Walls press in on you,
Crushing any hope of escaping.
Glare of blinding sunlight.
Sun is rich, like yellow buttercups.
Sky is full of ideas and the ideas never end; like the sky.
That line of trees holds new things beyond.
Birds respect you as nature,
As soon as you step outside.
Walls are absent, you could reach out and
Your fingertips would only grasp open air.

Annie Hedger (15)
Inveralmond Community High School, Livingston

Burma Cyclone - Haiku

Bodies in water,
Wind howling in the distance
Why is there no help?

David Henderson (14)
Inveralmond Community High School, Livingston

The Tsunami

One swish of the wave and the car was hurtling down the street,
Like a boat in trouble out in the middle of the ocean,
The screams were deathly,
The cries were sore,
The force of this thing, this tsunami,
It was as strong as 100 of the world's strongest men,
The look of sheer pain and utter fear on everyone's faces,
Mothers grabbing their children, pulling them to safety,
Others clinging to trees and railings,
Anything they could grab quick enough and,
Hanging on for dear life.

Sarah Spence (15)
Inveralmond Community High School, Livingston

Tsunami

T errible lashing waves,
S treaming towards us,
U nless I can stop it,
N o chance of survival,
A ll the time death gets closer,
M any people will die,
I will now join them.

Andrew Robertson (15)
Inveralmond Community High School, Livingston

Cyclone - Haiku

An eye for a storm
Creation of the heavens
But nowhere to go.

Cameron Fulton (14)
Inveralmond Community High School, Livingston

War

War is deadly and vicious,
As a bunch of lions brutally attacking,
Tanks and weapons are raging,
Running through the streets and towns.

Guns and battles everywhere -
The war consumes both day and night,
There is no rest, no escape,
No hope left for the innocent.

War is hateful and destructive,
People, young and old, are killed,
Young men are sent into the tornado,
And then scattered lifeless on an alien shore.

Lewis Gorman (12)
Inveralmond Community High School, Livingston

The Tsunami

It's a devastating attack,
It kills millions of people,
It destroys houses,
Plants sweep away,
Young people dying,
Mothers crying,
The wave hits the land like a bomb
And spreads like lava,
Plague spreads too like bloody gore,
There is no electricity,
There is no clean water,
There is no help,
There are no more screams.

Michael Athanaselis (14)
Inveralmond Community High School, Livingston

Green Shine

The Earth green, bright and lush,
But the Earth seems to be dawning a flush,
Black, grey and many clouds of smoke,
But we can keep this at bay.

Walking around, riding a bike,
These are the things that will make the green shine,
Through dull dark days of death and crime.

Letting trees grow, oak wood and pine,
These are the trees that will make the green shine.

Follow these rules and the land will bloom red, white and blue,
These are the colours that make the green shine through.

Alexander Leek (13)
Inveralmond Community High School, Livingston

Hope

People killing, people dying, children hurt and
You hear them crying, all is silent, all is still,
Soldiers ordered shoot to kill, told to fight till there's no will,
Songs and prayers sent up above,
Only he'll give them love . . .

Shaun Cotgrave (13)
Inveralmond Community High School, Livingston

Untitled

The world's people have nowhere to put their waste,
Except into the surrounding sea and countryside,
The animals, the people are losing their lives,
The world is wearing away,
The streets and our houses have become junkyards,
The rivers and oceans have become our drains.

Piles and piles of junk a day,
The world has become our dustbin,
So reduce, reuse, recycle,
To stop this vicious cycle.

Jordan Laing (14)
Inveralmond Community High School, Livingston

War

War is terrifying for people in the army and out,
War is killing innocent people,
War is making people homeless,
War is leaving our town in such a mess.
War is making the world an unsafe place,
War is making this world an unhappy place,
War families crying when they hear their loved ones dying,
War is noisy as tanks open fire,
War is people going missing as they get held hostage,
War is the road to oblivion.

Scott Moffat (14)
Inveralmond Community High School, Livingston

Pollution

The sky has gone dark,
The ocean is crying,
I don't understand why all the pollution?
What's that I see?
I cannot believe in what I am seeing!
The world needs our help!
We need to stop tree cutting,
No more rubbish dumping,
We've gotta start thinking.

Connor Locke (13)
Inveralmond Community High School, Livingston

Homelessness

People in the streets, hungry with no food,
Babies crying for their mothers, they get no reply,
Lying on the streets where they're going to die.

On the streets it is cold, the homeless are grey,
The people have no hope because they are hungry.

People walk past them, like they are not there,
Hanging on tightly so they don't go up in the air.

Natasha Baker (13)
Inveralmond Community High School, Livingston

Our World Needs Our Help!

It is dark and gloomy, the pollution is spreading,
People are dying and children are crying,
The water is black and the fish are dying,
The sky is like a shadow is hanging over it,
The clouds are as dark as a raven's wing,
We don't know what to do, people are screaming.

We need to stop driving so much
And the sky will be beautiful again,
We need to stop throwing our rubbish away
And animals and plants won't lie,
We need to help each other so people don't die,
We need to recycle to save the world and our rainforests.

Richard Steel (13)
Inveralmond Community High School, Livingston

Pandas

P lease don't kill pandas,
A nimals are getting killed,
N ot a lot of animals are living,
D on't harm them,
A nd they will live.

Rebecca Black (16)
Merkland School, Kirkintilloch

Waste

Don't use cars,
Their fumes are dirty,
Walk and cycle,
A lot more,
Only fly if the country is far,
If it's not, take a boat,
Smoke comes out of factory chimneys,
Caused by coal and gas and oil,
Only use it if you really need to,
People shop way too much,
It's not really good for our planet,
We should buy less,
Recycle more,
And only buy what we really need.

Lauren Black (16)
Merkland School, Kirkintilloch

Litter, Litter Everywhere

Litter, litter everywhere, on the stairs, on the floor,
Litter, litter everywhere, around the house, on the streets,
Litter, litter everywhere, on the grass, in the ponds,
Litter, litter everywhere, through the sewers, into the rivers,
Litter, litter everywhere, on the beaches, in the sea,
Litter, litter everywhere, on the planet, into space,
Litter, litter everywhere, in our galaxy, throughout the universe.

Matthew Hutton (15)
Merkland School, Kirkintilloch

Child Abuse

From inside the house there comes a scream,
What happens inside there must be mean,
I look to the window and here's what I see,
A bruise-covered child looking at me,
That innocent child hurt and scared,
His parents turn and they stared and glared,
They shut the curtains but still I could peep,
Their child, a prisoner, in their keep.

I walk away, my head filled with rage,
If that's first, what's the next stage?
For these abused children, there's not enough done,
No light, enjoyment, even no fun,
They don't feel safe in their own home,
They're not free to walk, run and roam,
This is an issue stuck in my mind,
It is now time for the parents to be kind.

It stops here, here today,
It is now time for the children to run and play.

Jessica Ames (12)
Lord Lawson of Beamish School, Birtley

Child Abuse Poem

It's not fair on children,
For them to be abused,
People leave their children confused,
Wondering what they've done wrong,
Hoping and praying it doesn't go on.

Hitting and kicking they don't deserve,
Bruises are left all over their bodies,
They try to have fun,
But they feel there's no sun.

Scared to come home,
Waiting alone,
Wish they were dead,
Marks left all over their head.

One girl is screaming from inside the house,
But that girl could never get out.

Jodie Hay (11)
Lord Lawson of Beamish School, Birtley

War Is Bad

War might not ever end,
In war you can never lend,
War means a lot of damage,
War does not mean doing homage,
War can be an outrage,
War sets you at a non-turnbackable stage,
War can really make you shout,
Sometimes you wish you wouldn't get put out,
War is when you are in rage,
War gets you put in a cage,
Even if you lend a hand,
You will be drowned in quick sand,
Lots of people die,
Their families wish they could say bye,
Most people cry,
But some people just give a short sigh,
War can be bad,
It will all come to you when you're sad.

Shawn Kurian (12)
Lord Lawson of Beamish School, Birtley

Good Will Come!

G reen grass soon to be black,
L itter always in attack,
O n the floor lying there,
B eing still without a care,
A lways people throw it down,
L iving mostly with a frown.

W ith warm and cold,
A nd lots of mould,
R eally it is very sad,
M aking it very bad,
I t hurts to say that,
N othing goes away and hopefully,
G ood will come!

Laura-Beth Loram (12)
Lord Lawson of Beamish School, Birtley

Terrorism

T is for terrorists who don't care who they hurt,
E is for everyone who is affected by this frightening event,
R is for rage that terrorists must be feeling,
R is for the roar of the bombs as they drop,
O is for orange, the colour of fire,
R is for red, the colour of danger,
I is for all of the invalids that are hurt by the bombs,
S is for the screams of people who get hurt,
M is for many people who have lost their lives.

Kate Patrick (12)
Lord Lawson of Beamish School, Birtley

Bullying

Scary and humiliating,
Upsetting and obliviating,
This makes me so furious,
How can people do this?
Hearts are breaking,
Lives can be taken,
This is so outraging!
Spoiling people's lives, it's sick,
How on Earth can people take the mick?
Hurting inside and outside too,
Could all of this be happening to you?
People have to take a loss,
This makes me really, really cross!
Not feeling safe, how upsetting,
I can't believe that this is happening,
Bullying must stop right now,
It gets people really down.

Emily Ramshaw (12)
Lord Lawson of Beamish School, Birtley

Animal Abuse

Animals' abuse happens each day,
Animal abuse will never go away,
Animals are scared to close their eyes,
Animals' hearts are all going to die.

Animals are left alone in the dark,
Animals are terrified and too scared to bark,
Animals are alone all night long,
Animals whimper a sad, lonely song.

Animals get strangled by the chain,
Animals go through so much pain,
Animals feel really tense,
We can help them for just 50 pence.

Rachel Reilly (12)
Lord Lawson of Beamish School, Birtley

Litter Streets

The bins are empty,
The streets are full,
This is bad,
The world is becoming a rubbish ball,
The world is a mess,
The streets are smelly,
When you walk out the door,
What do you meet?
A crisp packet in the middle of the street,
This makes me disgusted,
The world is now like this,
Save the world now,
Before it's too late.

Bethany Sanderson (11)
Lord Lawson of Beamish School, Birtley

Recycle

Keep it clean,
Keep it green,
All of us must work as a team.

Walk to school,
Ride a mule,
All of us must always think green.

Pick up litter,
Don't feel bitter,
All of us must work as a team.

Use the bin,
Watch your skin,
All of us must always think green.

Liam Anderson (12)
Lord Lawson of Beamish School, Birtley

Recycle

The recycle robot loves his job,
He tidies the Earth,
Even his body is recycled,
His head is a broken computer,
His nose is three tin cans,
His mouth is a keyboard,
Teeth the keys,
His ears are giant broken mirrors,
His body's a washing machine,
The robot's neck is a giant spring,
Arms and legs metal scraps,
With wooden feet and chopping board hands,
He recycles the Earth.

Amy Cowen (12)
Lord Lawson of Beamish School, Birtley

Stop Litter, It Is A Crime!

Every time you hear the church bell chime,
Just think it is time,
Litter is rubbish, litter is crime,
Litter is something not in time.
Drop litter if you want a £50 fine,
There are rubbish bins here and there,
So use them if you don't mind!
If you don't put litter on the bus,
It is not much work for us.

Nicole Nunn (11)
Lord Lawson of Beamish School, Birtley

Green

Keep the world clean,
Go for green,
Don't litter, it's just not cool,
Get out of the car and walk to school,
Think before you make that choice,
We all must speak with one clear voice.

Thomas Richardson (12)
Lord Lawson of Beamish School, Birtley

If You Were Me!

If you were me,
You would surely see,
Rainforests so green,
That once could be seen,
Passing my door is an empty bus,
While men with their cars make lots of fuss,
Have a taste,
Of your smelly waste,
Animals and extinction,
What are we thinking?

Stacey Sangster (12)
Lord Lawson of Beamish School, Birtley

The Solution To Pollution

Keep it green, keep it clean,
Save your power, don't waste it for hours,
Stop pollution, think up a good solution,
Save your light, you all know it's right,
Get the gas out the air, just show the Earth you care,
Put your litter in the bin,
Don't be bitter, make your planet fitter,
The Earth will be healthy one day,
Just keep pollution at bay.

Alex Terry (12)
Lord Lawson of Beamish School, Birtley

Rules

Trees are green,
Red roses too,
The noise of rivers,
Gives you shivers.

Leaves fallen off trees,
People go on shopping sprees,
Littering all over,
There should be rules about the four-leaf clover.

Ross Webb (12)
Lord Lawson of Beamish School, Birtley

You Do It!

You put the litter on the floor,
Don't do it and instead think more,
You drive to school in a big car,
So walk in future, it's not far.

You smash bottles in your angry state,
Stop and think of ways to create,
So come on people, let's make a stand,
Let's not destroy this stunning land.

All the forests that are long gone,
Along with all the animals and birds that no longer have a song,
If we continue in this way,
There will be nowhere for children to play,
We have to change now each little bit so
Come on everybody,
You can do it!

Rosie Young (12)
Lord Lawson of Beamish School, Birtley

War

Why kill to make the world a better place?
Make peace and be good,
Killing is sad,
What would you do if your dad or son, husband died?
Won't you be sad?
People go to other countries for making peace,
All they do is risk their lives to make peace to the world,
Just try to get along,
Think about your family when you are killing innocent lives.

Akash Balaggan (12)
Lord Lawson of Beamish School, Birtley

Environment

Pick things up, just be kind,
I know you don't want to be fined,
Each time when cars go by,
Pollution is invading, this is no lie.
Rainforests were very tall,
Now they are only small.
Each animal really counts,
Please don't be litterlouts.
Racism is a bad thing,
Put it away with a little *ping!*
Please listen and listen well,
The environment is an important place,
So will you help us Eco-kids?

Megan Berry (12)
Lord Lawson of Beamish School, Birtley

War

Young people at war, it is a shame to think of all of those lives lost,
Why can't they all make up?
There is bombing, shooting, so shocking,
Who would set out to hurt somebody?
All those lives lost, it is such a shame,
All they wanted is to make the world a better place,
All the families left with the disappointment of not having a
Dad, a son, or a husband,
They could have said no but they wanted to be counted.

Kirsty Cranney (11)
Lord Lawson of Beamish School, Birtley

Bin!

Rubbish in the street,
Covers our feet,
All over the town,
Makes me frown,
Help's on the way,
It's on another day,
When you walk across the road,
Stop!
Think about how we live,
It's time for us to give,
Something back to our world,
Just stop!
Use a bin,
Don't be dim.

Megan Haswell (12)
Lord Lawson of Beamish School, Birtley

Litterbug

We love to walk, we love to run,
We chat and we play, it's so fun,
We eat our food and that's OK,
But don't just drop it, put it away,
We don't need to litter,
Don't be bitter,
When you walk, pick up that litter,
Put it in the bin,
Don't do a sin, just put it in a bin,
Flick on that light and don't be dim,
We won't walk, we won't sit here,
'Cause we will be in other people's litter,
If you drop, it won't be right,
Get to the bin, it won't bite,
Don't do a sin, just put it in the *bin!*

Liam Hopkins (12)
Lord Lawson of Beamish School, Birtley

Rainforests

A rainforest is full of creatures,
Creatures great and small,
Blue sky, buzzy bees and trees that are so tall,
But the trees are getting chopped down,
And the creatures are all dying,
We must help them quick,
Come on, you're not even trying,
I know you might not care,
But this is really bad,
Please just help or the animals will be sad,
So please help our *eco-kids!*

Beth Stanger (11)
Lord Lawson of Beamish School, Birtley

Make A Change To Life!

'Keep your rubbish until you get to a bin!'
My mum always says,
Don't throw litter in the streets,
There's a dog that died the other day,
Down in Can's Alley,
He couldn't take the pollution anymore,
He unfortunately choked and died,
So help clean up your act,
Don't do the crime and stay out of doing it,
Help others to create a better world,
Recycle: The possibilities are endless!

Abbie Stoneman (11)
Lord Lawson of Beamish School, Birtley

Homeless

I live in a box,
I wear no socks.

I live on the street,
And itch my feet.

I have no money,
I have no home.

My mum and dad,
Left me on my own.

I walk the street
And hurt my feet
And now I live alone.

I want to be safe
And have a family,
But that will never happen.

Kyle Barnes (12)
Lord Lawson of Beamish School, Birtley

War

Bombs going off, everyone knows what's going on,
Guns going off all day long, no one knows who's really gone,
As there is gunfire, who knows who dies and who survives,
It's still going on, who knows who's gonna go on and win,
We're going down one by one, there is no hope,
Who's gonna go on and win?
Will I get back and be free for all eternity?
War, war no more, everyone change the law
And war will be no more.

Jamie Carr (12)
Lord Lawson of Beamish School, Birtley

Homeless

Nowhere to stay,
That's not OK,
Chucked out,
As my mam and dad shout,
'Never come back again!'

I am going insane,
My life is a pain,
I am always cold,
No one to hold.

People call me a tramp,
Only light is a street lamp,
I would like a place that is warm,
Please find me a humble home,
A place to call my own.

Devon Parkin (11)
Lord Lawson of Beamish School, Birtley

What Is Abuse?

Pets are pets,
People are people,
But abuse should be banned.

Pets are pets, loving and gentle,
Not to be starved,
All they see in their owner's eyes is hatred.

Pets are pets, loving their walks,
People are people, too lazy to walk,
All that they see is an unloving owner.

Pets are pets too ill to live,
People are people, too lazy to take them to a vet,
All that they see is death.

Caitlin-Leigh Rogers (11)
Lord Lawson of Beamish School, Birtley

In The Dark Black Valley

In the dark black valley is where I sleep,
In the dark black valley is where I eat,
In the dark black valley is where I live,
In the dark black valley is what I put up with.

Alone in the world, no family, no friends,
I ruined my life with a stupid bet,
I lost all my money, even my home,
Now I'm left with nothing, not even some clothes.

In the dark black valley is where I suffer
In the dark black valley is where I freeze,
In the dark black valley is where I live,
In the dark black valley is where I starve.

On my own I celebrate alone,
My birthday,
Christmas,
Even Easter,
I beg for money as people pass by,
Nothing though, just some stones off the ground.

In the dark black valley there comes a light,
In the dark black valley I hope it's my rescue,
In the dark black valley I'm left alone,
No breath, no life, no nothing,
Not anymore.

Zoe Sutton (12)
Lord Lawson of Beamish School, Birtley

Pete Has Lost His Home

There was a man,
Who was banned,
From his house,
And all he had was a tiny pet mouse.

He lived in the street,
In a cardboard box
And his name was Pete.

'I wish my wife,
Did not kick me out
And it feels like,
The end of my life.'

Daniel Neil Walker (11)
Lord Lawson of Beamish School, Birtley

Bomb, Bomb, Fifty Thousand Gone

War, war is knocking at your door,
Run upstairs and grab your M4,
Next thing you know, bye-bye door,
One bomb, the whole block gone,
Can't find my children and dust covers the sun,
My life is done, now I'm going to kill someone,
Calm down, no need to argue, please stop the fight,
Bomb, bomb, fifty thousand gone.

Dominic Davis (11)
Lord Lawson of Beamish School, Birtley

How To Make The World A Better Place

The world is a *bad* place,
The world is a sin,
Sometimes I wish I could live in a bin.

The world has war,
The world has litter,
It makes me feel so, so bitter.

Bullying is spreading around,
Racial abuse, horrible comments
These things are so not sound.

There are people who are fighting for us,
There are animals that are getting killed,
And there are people who can hardly build.

People think it's clever but really it's not,
People get injured,
And sometimes even shot.

That's not what we want, you know it's not,
Let's just change
It will be worth a lot.

Our world should be different,
And we can make that happen,
When it's a better place, we'll all be laughing.

Hannah Gomersall (12)
Meols Cop High School, Southport

Environment Poem

Environmentally friendly, that's what I am,
Doing my bit for the Earth,
Recycling, recycling, doing what I can,
Doing my bit for the Earth.

Pollution, pollution; it's a deadly gas,
Causing global warming,
Factory chimneys blowing out the mass,
We're not seeing the warnings.

Can we fix it if we pull together?
Everyone must change their habits to succeed,
New start and new ways can only get better,
If the government makes its mind up we can proceed.

It's too late, it's too late,
All we can do is wait,
Time's run out, time's run out,
It's going to be our fate.

Alan Jameson (12)
Meols Cop High School, Southport

Green Issues

E veryone listen up,
N otice the world around you,
V ery few trees are surviving,
I t's because of you and me,
R eally we need to *stop!*
O therwise our rainforests and creatures will die,
 Nature as we know it will no longer be for the future
  generations to see,
M ake a promise today and don't throw it away,
E nvironment, environment, save the environment,
N early everyone is trying to save the environment, why don't you?
T ake my advice and start today!

Cally Mannering (12)
Meols Cop High School, Southport

Why?

Leaning on the iced barriers, parting me from the lake,
I am wondering.
Rainbows, surrounding the icy lake and mountains,
like guardian angels.
As I watch them fade, bringing back the meaning of my mission.
'Save the world,' the words running through my head.
Turning my head, I see on the horizon:
Carts, trucks, wagons and motorbikes
Blurring down the highway, desperate to reach their destination.
Distant rumblings tell nature to be strong,
... A giant is coming.
Dark swirling clouds cover the still ocean,
Closer and closer they come.
The wind is screeching through the treetops.
Thunder, lightning is all that comes.
Rain follows in unison.
I am wondering why,
Why would mankind want to destroy such a beautiful sight?

Jennie Bartley (13)
Meols Cop High School, Southport

What's Wrong?

To this world, we have brought nothing but trouble,
Here and there and everywhere,
We have to do something to right our wrongs,
Or the world will end soon,
Round up pollution by picking up litter,
Let's stop pollution,
And make this a better place for everyone.

Keith McDonald (12)
Morogoro International School, Tanzania

Our World

Global warming isn't hard to explain,
It leaves us with excruciating pain,

This hurts our planet in every way,
This will make us have to pay,

Carbon dioxide is destroying the ozone layer,
You need to show you care,

We need to try and do our best,
Mother Nature needs to rest,
Our planet is precious and can't be replaced,
We need to act now or we will be erased.

Amancio Gomes (12)
Morogoro International School, Tanzania

A Poem About Pollution

P eople pollute the world,
O xygen is what we inhale,
L itter is spoiling the world,
L ife is getting worse,
U nhealthy for us,
T he world is coming to an end,
I hate pollution,
O ur atmosphere is at stake,
N obody admits their mistake.

Maitham Rajvani (11)
Morogoro International School, Tanzania

What Is Poverty?

Poverty is life
With no house or food;
No education
For some there is no hope.

Human greed:
That's what causes poverty.
We should think of others
Not only ourselves.

Let's all wake up,
See what we are doing
To our brothers and sisters,
All because of greed.

There is so much poverty
In the big world out there
And some are living in hopeless despair.
I'm scared poverty is going to take over the world
We should stand up and act for:
'Charity begins at home'.

Saskia Gomes (13)
Morogoro International School, Tanzania

Global Warming

Global warming
is causing
a lot of destruction.

It leaves Mother Earth
crying in grief and pain.
These changes could leave us
in sorrow and dismay.

The temperature is rising,
day by day.
The glaciers are melting,
and going away.

Soon everything will be gone,
if we don't start helping now,
in some or other way.

We are murderous killers,
destroying our magnificent Earth,
But no one is understanding,
some are just pretending.

Mother Nature can't do it all,
so let's give her a chance.

Our Earth is precious,
and it can't be replaced.
If we don't act now,
then our world will be erased!

Ayushi Maheshwari (14)
Morogoro International School, Tanzania

Humans Are Murderers

Butterflies flying,
Birds chirping,
Animals playing,
Humans will kill them all!
From the cutest to the ugliest,
From the strongest to the weakest,
From the tallest to the shortest,
Humans will kill them all.
Why ruin and kill creatures?
Why burn fuel and use cars?
Why ruin the next generation's future?
One day we will find ourselves lost,
Lost in the universe of our minds,
Not knowing what to do.
Having spoiled our homes, the Earth.
We make our future,
What we do now will decide our destiny,
Save energy now.

Noel Nnyiti (14)
Morogoro International School, Tanzania

Earth

I am planet Earth
I am strong
I can carry millions of people
I am full of air
Therefore the people don't care
They destroy my beautiful environment by littering
A long time ago I was really beautiful
But people just now are not careful
They are destroyers of Earth.
The trees were free
And the air was as light as a feather
I was shining with bright light
But now it is always night
I was clean like a whistle
All day, all night
Do not destroy Earth
It is as beautiful as a rose.

Farhan Bhanji (13)
Morogoro International School, Tanzania

Litter - Haikus

We drop our litter
But birds' food is not litter.
Animals do die.

Bins overflowing,
Waste pouring through alleyways,
Wind spreading rubbish.

Litter doesn't help,
Someone does try to clean it,
Though that's not enough.

Joe Michael (12)
Robert Mays School, Odiham

Environment Poem

Fire, fire burning bright,
In the forest of the night.
How could one so brave and kind
to let the forest keep its night
Now I'm telling you the climate story,
of why our planet is suddenly warming.
Our seas, our rivers, our land
which we are poisoning,
with our toxins and waste,
which we are pouring,
into every space and crevice
we can find.
What is going through our mind?

Aimee Hall (11)
Robert Mays School, Odiham

Be Grateful

When you are alone
and you feel so sad
but you don't know what to do,
you think of all those homeless people
who have nothing of what you have.
Homeless people have only clothes and
fire in a bin.
But people who are not homeless
have money, clothes and electricity.
Homeless are poor, but you may not be.

Emily Ward (12)
Robert Mays School, Odiham

Danger Of Extinction!

Extinction is all because of greed,
Our children might never see,
A creature roaming freely.

Out there in oceans deep,
Somewhere in forests dark,
The sound of a gun,
For the animal the world goes black!

Children won't know a whale song,
Or see an eagle gliding through the sky.
Appreciate a deer's beauty,
Or listen to wolves howl.

Without God's creatures, Mother Earth would be nothing,
Protect them now from extinction,
Don't wear a real fur coat,
And maybe for tomorrow's child they might see,
A creature roaming freely in the wild . . .

Eirin Cowle (11)
Robert Mays School, Odiham

Homeless

The night is dark,
The moon is cold.
Staring at me, crippled and old.
Homeless now,
Homeless forever.
My time has come,
I'm ready to fly away.
Moving on,
It's been forever, and a day.

Bethany Bleathman (12)
Robert Mays School, Odiham

War Of Mysteries

Where did they come from?
Why do they do it?
Who sent them?
I guess we will never find out.
We were gone before the end of night,
No one was left by the rising of the sun.
And then every day it would happen again,
The same old story.

Joe Laker (12)
Robert Mays School, Odiham

Animal Poem

Cheetahs, tigers, rhinos too,
Now it's all come down to you.
Can you stop the world from dying
Or will you sit there and start crying?

Peter Wernham (12)
Robert Mays School, Odiham

Wrong

Dolphins, pandas and lions were eating,
Then hunters shot them,
It's wrong.
Hunters create extinction every day.
Animals are always killed, it's wrong.

Shannon Kelley (12)
Robert Mays School, Odiham

Homeless

Why so cold?
Why so lonely?
Why so unsafe?
I'm homeless,
No family,
No friends,
No home,
I'm homeless.

Alexandra Davies (12)
Robert Mays School, Odiham

Eco-Friendly

E veryone needs to help
C all the world, it's waiting
O bviously, needs our help.

F riendly is what we need to be
R ecycle
I rritated is the world
E ver heard of a word called *green*?
N ever heard of a word called green!
D en you better start listening
L ove your world
Y ou can help!

Jennifer Harwood (12)
Roundhay School Technology College, Leeds

Inconvenient Fruit

I am smelling car fumes,
The car fumes from that beautiful Lamborghini,
I am seeing change,
Change in the town, the country, the world.
I am feeling the heat,
The heat of rays that lull me into a false utopia,
I am tasting big red strawberries,
Strawberries which are juicier than I remembered,
It dawns on me, maybe these changes
are more deceptive than we think.
The strawberries are being better grown
as a result of the amount of sun.
The car fumes are increasing by the day.
Watch out!
The future's about.

Marie Williams (12)
Roundhay School Technology College, Leeds

Happy Earth Day

If we keep damaging our Earth,
Greenhouse gases and climate change,
What will it be worth?
Global warming isn't strange,
It's ruining our Earth.

Switch off the light,
Turn off the water,
At morning and night,
It's just a small gesture,
The temperature is rising.

Recycle your rubbish,
Paper, plastic and metal,
Get the waste to the finish,
Don't let it get any more crucial,
Climate change is happening.

If you get involved,
Together with our friends,
We can get this problem solved,
Not just at the weekends,
Global warming is an issue.

Hannah Butland (13)
Roundhay School Technology College, Leeds

If Only . . . If Only . . .

If only people would turn off lights,
Stop cutting down trees,
Didn't waste water,
The world would be a better place.
If they recycled paper,
And walked to places,
Instead of driving,
The world would be a better place.
If no litter was dropped,
No seas were polluted,
The world would be cleaner, healthier and better.

Evie Spiridon (13)
Roundhay School Technology College, Leeds

The World

Before:
The world is a beautiful place, *unique*
In its own way
Amidst the gardens, flowers grow, *beautiful*
In its own way
And in the rivers, fish swim, *stunning*
In its own way.

After:
And in the factories smoke bellows, *disgusting*,
In every way.
And in the forest trees cut down, *disgusting*
In every way.

Make the world a better place.

Alhassan Dalghous (12)
Roundhay School Technology College, Leeds

Our Desperate Planet

Some people say we've left it too late
Our wasteful lifestyles have sealed our planet's fate.
The clock is ticking and the ice caps are melting,
Soon the heat will be too hot to bear; it will be sweltering
Recycle, cut back, walk instead of drive
These are some of the things we need to do to survive.
All the governments should act, no more arguing and debates.
Tough rules throughout the world before it is too late.

Beth Holdsworth (13)
Roundhay School Technology College, Leeds

Dream Of A World

Dream of a world with no pollution,
A world with an upheld constitution;
Thou who shalt litter,
Shall suffer the consequences; harsh and bitter.

Dream of a world without plastic bags,
Where green is the colour of all our flags.
Cars are a truly awful thing,
Without them on the road we could all sing:

We need not dream anymore,
The world has completed its chore.
The sky is lovely and blue;
Not full of grey, how can this be true?

Joseph Hudson (13)
Roundhay School Technology College, Leeds

Eco-Poem

We are destroying our planet,
Why can't we just ban it?
Attacking our Earth with greenhouse gases,
Killing our world for the masses!
We are doing this bit by bit!
Don't litter! Don't fly tip!
So listen now and take the hint,
You must reduce your carbon footprint!
Recycle and reuse it,
But please don't abuse it!

Christopher Pearce (13)
Roundhay School Technology College, Leeds

The Litterers

Strange little creatures,
treading all around,
when they have litter,
they throw it on the ground.

Other little critters,
have habits tidying,
and when they see some litter,
they throw it in a bin.

I don't know if you've noticed,
It's plain as you can see,
that all these little animals,
are simply you and me!

If none of us drop litter,
the better the world will be,
and everyone will all join
hands and . . . *shout out happily!*

Isobel Foster (12)
Roundhay School Technology College, Leeds

Find A Solution

Find a solution
To stop the pollution
Just try to recycle
Forget about the car and just cycle
Find a solution
To stop the pollution
Save the ozone
And please don't moan
Find a solution
To stop the pollution.

Stuart Forrester (13)
Roundhay School Technology College, Leeds

The Solution To Pollution

The solution to pollution
Is our revolution
Dropping litter is so bitter
Put the light out before your night out
Don't go in the car if it's not that far
Don't stand in the shower for more than an hour
If we just ignore it
We *will* destroy it.

Beth Elston (13)
Roundhay School Technology College, Leeds

What Can We Do?

The ice caps are melting
What can we do?
People are dying
What can we do?
Countries are flooding
What can we do?
The atmosphere's melting
What can we do?
Let's face the situation
And not run away
Solve the problem
Not tomorrow, today.

Edward Bennett (13)
Roundhay School Technology College, Leeds

Bin It Or Burn Us

Help our cities, help our towns.
They are in danger of crashing and burning.
Can *you* hear the sounds?
Crying for help, our world is yearning,
We must *stop* now or all will be lost.
Why won't you join in?
Or human lives will be the cost.
So recycle your rubbish or use a *bin!*

If we all work together and start really trying
Then soon our world will be *great!*
Saving our planet will stop all the crying
So start working *now!* And stop all the hate.
We can save our world and all living creatures
It'll help no end and save our *lives*
So we can enjoy our world's beautiful features
Our planet will have balance and no more strife.

Oliver Watson (13)
Roundhay School Technology College, Leeds

Rainforest

R ainforests disappearing every day
A lways think of others and how they feel
I n every person there is freedom
N ow find your heart to help the rainforest
F ight against the poverty we are creating
O thers need our help to keep their lives going
R ise against the cruelty of animals
E veryone contribute to help the death of others
S ave the animals from extinction
T ake action to keep the rainforest.

Rachael Jones & Nicole Millington (12)
Roundhay School Technology College, Leeds

Reduce Your Carbon Footprint!

Reduce your carbon footprint
Don't fly around the Earth
Don't leave your landing lights on
Recycle for all you're worth.

Reduce your carbon footprint
Don't cut down all the trees
Don't use your central heating
And only eat local peas.

Reduce your carbon footprint
Don't use plastic bags
We've got to make a difference
And I don't mean to nag.

Gwenna Hare (12)
Roundhay School Technology College, Leeds

Questions

Must it go on
These endless wars
That are tearing apart families
And destroying land?
How many more people
Will be killed
Before the governments realise
How much distress they are causing?
Don't people think
Before they launch into attack?
Do they think about the families
Whose homes and lives have been destroyed?
Does anybody have the answers?
Does anybody know?
Then tell me please
What is the point of war?

Emily Richardson (11)
Roundhay School Technology College, Leeds

A World Of Difference - Poems From The UK And Around The World

Why?

Why do people drop litter
Which makes them all so very bitter?
Pick it up, put it in the bin,
Now you know it's not a sin.
Why do people pollute the Earth?
Why don't we treat it for what it's worth?
Stop the cars, stop the trains,
Why don't we just use our brains?
Why do animals have to go through that pain?
Are we humans all insane?
Save the animals, save the trees,
Stop it, save it, help it *please!*

Ravi Rathore (12) & Saif Ishafaq (11)
Roundhay School Technology College, Leeds

Animal Extinction

All for us
Wildlife's homes chopped down
Just for us
Just for paper

All for us
Hurricanes, floods
Tsunamis, losing animals
Just for us.

Think about
Polar bears, leopards
Suffering without food
All for us.

So think about what you're doing!

Jasmine Baker & Jenny Watson (11)
Roundhay School Technology College, Leeds

Daddy's Gone Out Today

Daddy's gone out today
He said he won't come home.
Mummy's been crying today
So I'm all on my own.

He took a rucksack with him
When he went out the door.
I've got my banner out now
But Mummy's fallen to the floor.

She's hitting the floor hard
She's crying, she's weeping.
She's talking nonsense and
Her make-up is streaming.

A man phoned today
He said Daddy's not coming home.
Mummy's still on the cold floor
So I'll make dinner on my own.

Daddy died today
Doing his fatal job.
Daddy is sleeping now
Along with Uncle Bob.

Rachael Matheson (12)
Roundhay School Technology College, Leeds

On The Kerb

On the kerb, here I sit,
In the air so cold and bitter,
Cast away like a piece of litter,
On the kerb, here I lie,
Have no friend and no home
In the world I am all alone.
On the kerb, here I stare,
Watching the world pass me by,
Some with pity, some with sighs,
If only they knew what I've been through,
If only they knew why I cry,
On the kerb, here I sit,
Till the day I die.

Elizabeth Gabriel (12)
Roundhay School Technology College, Leeds

The Future

A barren wasteland
Overwhelms what was once green
Natural debris

Dried up seas and rivers
Make foul craters in the Earth
Causing much danger

Many don't survive
The harsh weather conditions
Due to CO_2

Or...

A blue sky shines down
To a grand Utopia
That we helped create

No global conflict
A thriving community
Working hand in hand

If we recycle
And help our environment
Through global warming

Then we can hope for
A brighter tomorrow.

Tessa Leggiero (12)
Roundhay School Technology College, Leeds

Why?

Our lush meadow seems never-ending,
The floodplain stretches far,
Sapphire sky drapes itself over the emerald hills.
Fragrant, soft breeze ripples the water,
Runs through the velvet hair of the grazing doe,
And tickles the whiskers of the field mouse.
The only tree sits next to the meander,
But it is not lonely.
The blue tits, wrens, chaffinch and thrush,
Sit and sing in its sturdy, protective arms.
Down by the long grass and the groups of bulrushes,
Ladybirds, tiny moths, bumblebees and dragonflies hop from,
One perfumed iris to another.
Rainbow gold sunlight shimmers off,
The silver scales of fish in the cool blue water.
Zzer, zzer, clink, clink,
Zzer, zzer, clink, clink.
What is this
Coming over the steep slope?
Who are they with yellow plastic things on their heads?
A growling, snarling giant with round feet is rolling down towards us,
It clanks and rattles, it is carrying weapons,
But they're not tooth and claw,
They're big, heavy, metal,
And indestructible.
No! No! No!
The round feet are tearing at the soft grass.
No! No! No!
The beings with yellow plastic things on their heads are cutting down the tree.
No! No! No!
Their giant scooper is filling in the river,
The thick, suffocating mud soaking up the source of life.
No. No. Oh, no.
They have ruined our paradise.
Enormous blocks of brick are making millions of new homes,
While ours have been destroyed.
Where can we go now?
The creatures of the meadow weep.

Our meadow seemed never-ending,
The floodplain still stretches far,
But now, it supports hollow houses,
Sad structures of stone,
The new occupants don't know what they have done.
Or do they?
You have made us homeless.
You have abandoned us to the harsh life outside of the meadow,
You have killed us.
Why?

Rosie Muncer (12)
Roundhay School Technology College, Leeds

The Environment

The environment is made up of
Rivers, oceans and seas,
Plants, flowers and trees,
Animals like cats and dogs,
Fish, insects and frogs,
Mammals, reptiles and birds,
All sorts of animals in their herds,
In the city there are thousands of cars,
Shops, restaurants and bars,
Factories releasing poisonous gases,
CO_2 increasing as the day passes,
Causing an increase of temperature to be felt,
And polar ice caps will melt,
This will cause a flood,
That will destroy our earth, soil and mud,
Oil will soon run out,
Then how will we survive without?
Unable to travel about,
We should try to be more green,
'Cause we're producing the most CO_2 this world has ever seen
We should respect our environment a lot,
After all, it is the only one we've got.

Rahil Abedin (12)
Roundhay School Technology College, Leeds

Eco Friendly

Eco-friendly, make it better
Eco-friendly, make it greener
Eco-friendly, make it easier
Eco-friendly, stop driving cars!
Eco-friendly, start walking places
Global warming - make it *stop!*

Jasrag Singh Lota (12)
Roundhay School Technology College, Leeds

Look . . .

Look, look at day,
Look at night.
What can you see?
I see the sun setting.
And the moon rising,
Once more.

Look, look to the past,
What can you see?
I see fumes burning,
Creatures dying,
Over the past years.

Now, look to the future.
What can you see?
I see creatures living in harmony,
Through the night,
Through the day,
Creatures surviving always.

Usmaan Mahmood (12)
Roundhay School Technology College, Leeds

The Environment Poem

The environment is a wonderful place,
The litter and waste it has to face.
Driving your cars, causing pollution,
If you start walking, that can be the answer to our solution.
Think of what you're about to do,
Keep the litter in your hand and think it through,
Imagine how it feels to be dumped on with litter,
Now you're thinking, don't you feel a bit bitter?
Recycling is a fantastic thing to do,
You can reuse it and make it into something new.

Emma Daniel (12)
Roundhay School Technology College, Leeds

My Eco-Friendly Poem

Eco-friendly, eco-friendly,
that's all I hear
Eco-friendly, eco-friendly
give it a cheer.

Eco-friendly, eco-friendly
keep our air clean
Eco-friendly, eco-friendly,
don't be so mean.

Eco-friendly, eco-friendly
remember to recycle
Eco-friendly, eco-friendly
so we can carry on our cycle.

Matthew Hayward (13)
Roundhay School Technology College, Leeds

Being Green

Why do people ruin the Earth?
Carelessly wasting the universe,
Can't they show some respect?
Because it's where we live
Why don't they care?
Why don't they help?
Why can't they be keen?
Why can't they be green?

If everyone does their little bit,
Being green would keep them fit,
By walking just that short way,
Instead of going by car that day
There are other ways of being green,
For instance, recycling things
So if every single person is keen,
Then we all will be green!

Helen Thompson (12)
Roundhay School Technology College, Leeds

A Warning

Oh the world was such a better place,
Before cars were invented,
Before toxic waste was dumped out of big scary buildings,
Before people liked to litter,
'Bio degradable!' They now say before tossing an apple core on the floor,
Oh the world!
What a wonderful place it was,
But people don't ever see that anymore,
The world is becoming a toxic wasteland,
Do something before it is too late,
This is your warning.

Shaan Sidhu (12)
Roundhay School Technology College, Leeds

The Time Is Now

I am not happy with what we have done
This is not for my life,
But for my children and theirs.

It is now that we have to change our ways
To grow aware
To save this planet and its beauty
For in its beauty is our survival
Let's tune into what's happening right now.

I was told in the Bible from God,
That we were masters of the planet,
We have betrayed God's word and his trust.

I think we should remember to love and care
And especially our responsibility.

It is time to change
Everything is counting on us.
I must change the planet for future generations . . .
So help me right now change this planet.

Savannah Acutt (12)
Ruzawi School, Zimbabwe

Deforestation, Pollution, Poaching And Global Warming - Haikus

Deforestation

Chopping down the trees
All the animals dying
Don't you feel ashamed?

Pollution

It's so disgusting
Big black clouds strolling around
It makes our lungs black.

Poaching

You may get the meat
But you are taking a life
Snares and traps are bad.

Global warming

The ice is melting
And the weather going wild
Will we burn up soon?

Sophie Hoard (11)
Ruzawi School, Zimbabwe

All Because Of Man

The screeching of a chainsaw.
The chopping of an axe.
Trees fall down with a terrible crash.
Animals die, birds' nests burn.
Once beautiful forests thick and green.
But now scorched earth.

Black oily rivers pass the city gates.
Animals die drinking at their edge.
Sewage runs from the homes to the oily depths of the river.
Killing rivers and seas with our waste.

Tigers' extinction is very close.
All Man wants is his striped coat.
Elephants' ivory, rhino horns.
The greed of Man taking from Earth.
And if you want our Earth to be a better place . . .
Open your eyes and look ahead before it's too late.

Emma Ball (11)
Ruzawi School, Zimbabwe

What's Happening To Our World?

The world is changing what shall we do?
With people being left homeless and animals too,
Forests are being burnt and nobody cares
Animals are killed by so many snares.
The trees are now stumps sliced by an axe,
And the jungles are left with many human tracks.

We took over this world many years ago,
Leaving so many species with nowhere to go,
Now look what's happened to the dodo,
Oh my goodness, where did he go?

We should look after our Earth
Every day in every way,
And that's what everybody should say,
Recycling our rubbish will go a long way,
If in this world we still want to stay.

Jason Hutchings (11)
Ruzawi School, Zimbabwe

A World Of Difference - Poems From The UK And Around The World

Pollution And Deforestation Haikus

Pollution

Rubbish, smoke and waste
Pollution is the problem
Stop polluting now

Deforestation

Deforestation
Destroys the animals' homes
Plant a tree today.

Amber Scott (12)
Ruzawi School, Zimbabwe

If I Could

If I could change this world
I'd like to hear no crying
And stop all war
I would see no ugliness
And have no racism
To have no people on the streets
To let everyone have the chance to eat.
For children to go to school
For all to have a home
For people to have friends and family to love,
And to be loved.
For everyone to unite together
And to form worldwide peace.

Julie Precious (11)
Ruzawi School, Zimbabwe

Mother Nature

Things are changing, Mother Nature's rhythm is broken,
Her heart weighs heavy, her soul is uneasy.
She struggles to breathe, is it all the smoke?
Where are all the trees? Oh please!
All of her creation respect and behave,
But for her thoughtless Man,
Greedy and ungrateful, he will drive her to her grave.
Spewing his poison, waste and littering his can.
The poisonous air makes her cry acid rain
The uncontrollable bush fire is her heart burning.
Her cyclone breath twists and twirls in savage pain.
Her tears fall and fall they turn to mud and then flood.
How this mother forgives and forgets, her selfish child.
Why oh why does she still love us?

Courtney Archer (12)
Ruzawi School, Zimbabwe

How To Save Our World

Conserve our lands
Stop cutting trees
Stop making cars
And save the bees.

Conserve our water
Stop industrial waste
Stop oil spills
And all with haste.

Conserve our wildlife
Save the beasts
And the flowers too
To do this is the least.

Michael Dodington (12)
Ruzawi School, Zimbabwe

Poverty And War Haikus

Sleeping in the streets
With no hope of salvation
In a bitter world.

No mercy, pain, strife
Only greed in people's hearts
Despair, death, revenge.

Takudzwa Mapupu (12)
Ruzawi School, Zimbabwe

Pollution

Exhaust fumes, smog and soot,
No one here seems to give a hoot,
The air used to be pure and clean,
Now it's smelly, dirty and mean.

Factories pump out a poisonous mix
The owners keep quiet about their dirty tricks,
Pollutants in the waters deep
Kill the creatures in their sleep.

The fluffy white clouds in the sky
Are disturbed by the jets, as they fly,
Millions of tonnes of dirty air
Pour out of their engines from year to year.

It's important for the world to think about tomorrow,
If we don't we will all ache with sorrow,
It's up to us to find a proper solution
To save our world from this evil pollution!

Rachel Hulett (12)
Ruzawi School, Zimbabwe

War Took My Home Away

I once had a home but war
came and took it away.

I was left in the dust to
choke on my own spite
in the rubble of my house.

At night I wander the streets counting
down the hours until the sun rises.

In the day I watch people go about
their daily lives.

I learned to be humble, kind and hopeful.
You long for your home, your sweet, sweet home.

People pity me but I say they shouldn't
for a big home is waiting for me,
with my father up in what's left of the big blue sky.

Feiyo-Peik Nghidinwa (15)
St Paul's College, Namibia

War

People are dying
Animals are dying
Nature is dying
And the world is crying.

What do we do?
It troubles me and you!
Blood is flowing and
No greens are growing.

As a student I face this
Sadness
In a country of total
Madness.

Why can't there just be
Peace?
Why can't everyone live at
Ease?

No more fighting
No more bombing
Let's hope that peace is coming.

Xenja Brown (14)
St Paul's College, Namibia

Poverty

Poverty is bad, it makes a lot of us sad.
No money for food but all they want is to be good
And go to school, but with no money, it's impossible.
No food, no water, no butter; that forces them to live in the gutter.
Poverty, the worst thing of all made most men fall,
But us men must still stand tall.

Uno Hinda (13)
St Paul's College, Namibia

Litter

I ask myself why people litter, maybe they are lazy or just being bitter,
But for our town to fly, we have to make an effort to try.

Wonder how people feel when they litter, bad, sad or glad?
Well I feel horrible because we're blessed with what we have today,
And it's ugly when people litter and they act like nothing happened that day.

For us to make a difference we have to work together to make our town a better place

And give God our grace.

Sally Salionga (13)
St Paul's College, Namibia

Pollution In Our Environment

Pollution is not worth,
It destroys Earth;

It makes the place look like a pile of mess,
Our happiness will be less;

Air, wind and land pollution,
Connect to destructive fusion;

Dirt makes the environment bad,
And makes us all feel sad;

We must try and stop pollution,
But first get a better imagination;

We have to work until we succeed,
So that our generations can proceed;

With our vision,
For our nation.

Tuki Jacobs (13)
St Paul's College, Namibia

Homeless

A lot are homeless,
Poor and hopeless.
Let us make a change today,
Let us stand together, yay!
Let us build a home,
For the homeless in the world
Provide food and school,
That's enough for them.
Heal their broken hearts with,
Comfort, love and care,
So that we can have,
A better world today!

Luche Feris (13)
St Paul's College, Namibia

A World Of Difference -Poems From The UK And Around The World

What Is Happening?

'The sun will be turned into darkness
And the moon into blood.'
Before us stretch forests of barrenness
We feel heat and stand in floods
Is the end already here?

'Inhabit, conserve and cultivate.' He said
But that rivals our fun
Murder, rape, so many already dead
Compassion there is none.
Who will take the plunge?

Factories, billow clouds of death
Missing are animals' songs
Increased reports of crimes and theft
The forests are all gone
What has happened here?

In darkness we have lost our faith
We've surrendered to death
We all wonder who'll be kept safe
When there's nothing left
What will happen?

If only we all did our proper part
Birth control, litter-free
Saving; it's the small things that end the dark
Is saving possible? Maybe
Where will we start?

Hope is blocked out by clouds of despair
Seeds of hate grow
If we would just give more and care
You can start the flow
What will you do?

I utter no words of accusation
But leave you with one last question
When will this end?

Anja Koekemoer (15)
St Paul's College, Namibia

Recycle

Our resources are almost gone.
We must act before we're done.
We can't afford to take the risk,
Because of this, I must insist
Recycle, reduce, reuse.
It is a need we can't refuse.
It is our world and we must save it.
Recycle, reduce, reuse.
It is a need we can't refuse.

Chelsea Petersen (14)
St Paul's College, Namibia

Open Your Eyes

When the sky is turning and moves the Earth,
If you and me may soon no longer exist
We wish to decide to consider and hope,
I dream and all options are open.

Can you see who you are?
Are you aware that it is
Every place
Every word
Every person
Everything is
Everything was
Everything is special.

Move and feel yourself
Make peace with yourself
Make peace with yourself and the Earth
The Earth is beautiful
Turn with her
You control every step
Move together
Make peace
Open your eyes
Make peace.

Just because I cannot see so many things
Does not mean that I cannot discover them
If I can share, what we are with you
I can learn
I'm alive
It's going on.

Karina Krönke (15)
St Paul's College, Namibia

Racism

Racism, what a powerful situation;
It's filled with such hatred and discrimination.
It has been a big issue for decades;
After being passed from generation to generation.
We ask ourselves who can end this?
But the answer lies with us.
We have to teach our children to love one another,
No matter the age, race, religion or gender.
Only we can change the ways,
The way of those who believe in discrimination.
So come on everyone let's stand together with determination,
To end this ridiculous situation.
Make a change, show the way,
Let us do it all today.
Racism, what a painful situation.
If we don't change the world today,
Who will tomorrow?

Nadia Simbi (14)
St Paul's College, Namibia

Racism

Racism is wrong, evil and bad
Let us not discriminate, but appreciate,
We should all participate . . .
In making our world a better place
For all the human race.
We should not see black or white,
Nor should we fight,
But we should all unite as *one!*

Daniel Mulongeni (15)
St Paul's College, Namibia

A Poem On Pollution

Dear friend out there, I'm writing this poem
To send out a message of my concern.

Have you my friend made a decision
On how to stop the cause of pollution
Perhaps you're reading and don't even care
But there are millions of people dying out there.

This struggle cannot be completed by two
We have to complete the race it's true
But this cannot be done without you
It starts with you and only you.

Millions of children are dying
While cigarettes we are buying
Animals are becoming extinct
In the poles they are about to sink.

Dear friend please hear my plea
We need to complete
The struggle of pollution
And you are the solution.

Pendukeni Pandeni (15)
St Paul's College, Namibia

Life

Life might be pleasant
Life might be tough
Throughout it we might grow tough.

Sometimes the skies are open and clear
But then they can be overcast and you feel fear.

As a thin tall tree withers in winter.
So it revives and shimmers in spring.

We have sunsets as pure as a ring of gold.
We have big, luscious green trees.
We have all types of animals going from A to Z.

But day by day these wonders are disappearing
Day by day they are falling away.

We do not see what is right in front of our eyes,
We do not see what is happening in the skies.
What was earlier overcast by thundering clouds
Is now overcast by thick pollution.

We must unite against this crime.
The crime of us allowing our planet to wilt away.
We should save it before we are too late.

Anita Janeke (14)
St Paul's College, Namibia

If We Work Together

Near or far climate has been changing,
Floods and famine have plagued our world.
Rain has come too early, too late, too much and too little,
Earth, a plentiful garden, is dying.

Wait, I see a dream, a hope,
If we're together now we might cope.
If we stop cutting down and burning fuel,
We could save Mother Earth.

Go home now, recycle what you can,
Plant some and burn less fuel.
If we do this it just might work,
You and me together.

Brook Eyob (11)
Sandford International School, Ethiopia

On The Streets

The poor children on the streets, begging for some cents:
I have no idea how they feel.
They don't want to think about dying.
But they know death is real.

Their bare feet on the freezing ground:
Screaming, *'Help!'* because they're in need of some warm love.
All they do is cry, beg and sometimes steal,
Or they get a cold and start to cough.

The blue tears drop out of their sad eyes,
And they wait for the graceful one, who gives them money.
For they do not know when or who,
For their only hope is a happy sunny day . . .

Lotte Driessen (13)
Sandford International School, Ethiopia

Loudest Cry Of All

She sings about the Earth
Like no one else has ever done so
She speaks so clear and pure
Of her heart beating slow
The fruits of her labour
Have been ripped from her soul
She cries with every life lost
She spins day and night
To keep us alive
She grows heavier with sorrow and death
And lighter with her life-giving breath
She sings with the wind and cries with the rain
No one seems to listen, no one seems to care
When our Mother Earth's heart bleeds storms and floods
Please, just listen.

Haimanot Haile (15)
Sandford International School, Ethiopia

Some Day, One Day

My father and brother
Went off to war
But never came back.
My mother and sister
Fell asleep but never woke up.
I was all alone in the world.
There were riots in the streets.
Fire burned and guns were fired.
Men yelled and women cried.
There's little rain or none at all.
There's not enough food to feed,
All the mouths on Earth.
Leaders cry to grow bio fuel.
But the people cry to grow more food.
The world perishes as the years go by.
The forests are gone and the animals have died.
One day, some day,
The world will sing in joy as the trees grow back
And the animals are born.
Some day, one day.

Tana Wambua Jupner (12)
Sandford International School, Ethiopia

What I See

When I look out the window what I see
All around me is poverty,
Not very far from the nice home I live in
Are dirty streets, beggars, tramps and orphans.
If lucky enough they might have a shack to stay in.

I go from place to place hearing songs of criticism,
All because of the fast growing wildfire of racism.
I hear and see racism between nations and skin colours
And people being disrespected because of the lack of dollars.

I think about all this
But a storm interrupts me.
I hear screaming and shouting
And the sound of guns shooting.
I take a gasp, it's my last breath,
For there's a gunshot and I face my death.

Tabo Chata (12)
Sandford International School, Ethiopia

A Lost Life

A life is lost,
But we don't care,
A disaster happens,
We stare in disbelief,
Half the world's forests are gone,
We still use it,
When it runs out,
It's a wake-up call for the world,
Maybe then we'll take actions,
But what actions,
It will be too late,
For the future generation.

Kalkidan Gezahegn (12)
Sandford International School, Ethiopia

Heal The World!

Peek in the future
The forests are gone
Trees only a memory
A distant heart's song
But he who plants a tree
Plants the staff of beauty towering high
The forest's heritage
The harvest of the coming age
Man is the vandal
Ripping their woods
For hundreds of years
Robbing what's good
Our skies once clear and blue
Now a coat of grey they wear
How can we turn our backs?
Ignoring nature's call
What about our children?
When there's nothing left at all
Let's stand hand in hand
Let's make mankind aware
'We must be the change, we wish to see the world'
Because the world is all that will remain!

Melat Fesseha Seyoum (15)
Sandford International School, Ethiopia

Senseless

We are blind
Not because we can't see what's around us
But because we refuse to.
We pretend to be deaf,
In reality we run
From our very own cries for help.
We inhale intoxicating fumes
As our ancestors once breathed in
The sweet smell of wild flowers.
We pollute and misuse our temples,
The human body,
We are spellbound and oblivious to the dangers.
Every man for himself,
We feel only for ourselves,
Ask yourself why.
Why we run from the truth and hide from the damage we've done.
We must stand together like an army,
Reach out to each other like long roots entwined.
We don't know that, alone we are weak,
Alone we are senseless.

Denisia Mangue (13)
Sandford International School, Ethiopia

A Better World

Deforestation, pollution and war are destroying our world.
Earth is one, we have no other place.
Stop being greedy, racist and careless.

We can start today, the tools are here.
Keep our neighbourhood clean.
We can use alternative energy,
Imagine a place where you can breathe fresh air,
Not smog and dirt.

Help others less fortunate,
Teach them to stand on their feet.
No more starvation, no more death or poverty!

Protect the animals from being extinct!
All of us can contribute to build a better world.

Angelica Astuti (12)
Sandford International School, Ethiopia

Revolution

Let's bring out the green peace,
To help our wonderful plants and trees,
To save the incredible nature,
So we can impress our creator.

Let's have a revolution,
To stop terrible pollution,
No more endangered animals going extinct,
So let's stop these horrible hunters from killing these things.

No more slave drivers and child labourers,
Stop being blind and let us be saviours,
Everyone should have a good education,
And access to every medication.

Why not have some love,
So that everybody could have enough?
There shouldn't be any differences between black and white,
And that's why I'm standing up for my rights!

Makeda Mitchell (12)
Sandford International School, Ethiopia

Poverty Made History

Blame it on the rich,
Blame it on the poor,
There's the thing you miss.

It was because of you and me,
Just as much as he and she,
One too much, one just over slight,
That's the cruelty facing us every night.

No roof or bed,
Nothing but their blood being shed,
Begging just before morning,
With the midnight gently clearing.

Another day means another chance,
To put an end to this lasting dance,
The spell cast upon the unlucky,
The fact of no food or money.

These are the facts I know,
The truths for the fortunate,
And words spoken for the unfortunate.

Moniek Haverkort (11)
Sandford International School, Ethiopia

Silence Of The Earth

The Earth is silent.
But inwardly crying, shouting out
For what we've done we are guilty
Yes we are, have you forgotten?
The millions of others we leave to rot?
The ones who live in fear day after day
Filled with hunger and sorrow
With so much to say.
The car that you buy today.
Will tomorrow kill that man
Who has to pay.
Is this not enough to make you see?
We have to change now, who knows what tomorrow will be?
Should we wait for the sky, once so blue and bright
To turn forever into the colour of night?
Or the air once so sweet and fresh
To carry with it the smell of death and decaying flesh,
How many more mistakes can we afford to make?
How much more time are we going to take?
The Earth will die,
Before we realise our mistake
We will stand there, lost for words
... The cycle of life will finally break.

Fikir Gezahegn (15)
Sandford International School, Ethiopia

Changing Lives

They're all living on the street, begging,
Feeding on hunger, sleeping on plastic bags,
Stealing but they're not proud,
They're suffering and dying.

They're catching diseases,
They're worrying where next to sleep,
They're always praying to have food and shelter,
But they're receiving hatred and disgust from people.

We're all the same, we're all people,
Shouldn't we take care of each other?
Costs have gone up,
This even makes it harder for them to live.

Some are drug addicts with no heart,
Some are abandoned children with no parents,
Some are sick with no shelter,
So let's think and change their lives.

Meriam Ture (12)
Sandford International School, Ethiopia

Rain Come Back

No rain today, neither tomorrow,
The crops are dying and we are starving.
We won't have any to sell or buy.
If there is no rain we'll be sure to die.
The rivers are drying up,
The animals are thirsty,
The cattle don't have enough to eat.
The climate is changing
And is making our lives harder.
Polluting must stop as well as deforestation.

Tsion Abraham (11)
Sandford International School, Ethiopia

Foresee And Forestall

21st century rolled in with its skaters,
Joining in the chain of life on nature.
Man exploits resources to be sustained,
Leaving our planet Earth in grave peril.
Economic, political and social factors,
Have led to an altered biosphere.
Expansion of gaps between rich and poor,
Has ripped apart our world.
Let us all fight against ignorance,
And bring change upon the natural environment.
Learn to come together as one,
To tackle the impact of humans on the planet.
Live and help live.
Foresee and forestall.

Amrot Assefa (15)
Sandford International School, Ethiopia

What is Poverty?

Poverty and I will never split up
With it in sight we will never grow up.
Poverty means hunger
Poverty means no leisure.
The rapid growth of poverty, the rapid loss of priority,
More and more poverty, less and less dignity.
Poverty means more refuge
Poverty means no shelter.
No need of warm jackets, a thin plastic will do,
No need of warm latte, a clean water will do.
Poverty means famine
Poverty means shortage in life.
In sickness and in health poverty won't stop,
For better or worse, poverty at the top.
Poverty means poorness.
Poverty means hardship.
Flood and drought, blame is on you,
So is war and greed too
Poverty is a long way home.

Eyerus Assefa (14)
Sandford International School, Ethiopia

Rain, Rain Everywhere!

R ain, rain everywhere,
A t any time the rain showers;
I n the city, in the village,
N o difference at all, not at all.
F lying dark clouds carry,
O ceans full of water droplets;
R emitting crystals of rain,
E verywhere, even on the mountains,
S ea, forest and all;
T rees swing with a melody in rain.

Michael Haileselassie (12)
Sandford International School, Ethiopia

I Feel Sad!

I feel sad that people are dying in poor countries.
I feel sad that no one will help them
But we have the power to help them.
I feel sad that people are becoming homeless
Day by day.
I feel sad that cruelty is going around Africa.
That's the thing, we humans only kill for fun!

Storai Ibrahim (13)
Slough Eton School, Slough

The Green Machine Eco-Kids

Throw your litter in the bin,
Don't commit the rubbish sin!
Bins are so neat and clean,
For the world's dirt that shouldn't be seen!

Recycle glass, clear, brown and green,
To make new bottles shiny and clean!
Recycling bottles and paper is good,
But we don't do it as often as we should!

Our animals, plants and nature are dying,
And litter is everywhere . . . and flying!
Plastic and tins are thrown everywhere,
Some thoughtless people just don't care!

What a shame we are not more careful,
We could end up with something dreadful!
Turn the world to green from brown,
It will wear a smile instead of a frown!

Olivia Philp (12)
Springvale House, Zimbabwe

My Violent And Polluted World

War is always on the news.
Violent bombs and radical views.
Seeing all the people die.
Just makes me want to cry and cry!

War tears countries and families apart.
It brings bad news and breaks one's heart.
Lasting peace is the only way.
We should help people day by day!

Global warming is affecting life.
Causing our Earth a great deal of strife!
Droughts and floods and rising seas.
Melting snowcaps and cutting down of trees!

Litter on streets and pollution in the air.
People of the world, do you not care?
We can make the world a better place.
So let's work together to win this race!

Ben Stijkel (12)
Springvale House, Zimbabwe

Cleaning Up Our World

Here is a very big solution,
For all this smelly, disgusting pollution,
Stop using deodorants that are ozone deadly,
Rather use roll-ons, which are ozone friendly.

Turn off the light when you leave the room,
Let's help avoid pollution's doom,
Rather walk than use your car,
And pollution will not get that far.

Start to use solar panels to help with light,
If we work together, we can win this fight,
Don't put rubbish into the sea,
Rather recycle it, you'll see what I mean.

The forest and animals are ours to take care,
If we want our children's children to see them there,
The world and its things are what we've been given,
Let's look after it, so it's worth the living.

Jessie Hough (12)
Springvale House, Zimbabwe

Saving Our World

Poverty is all around,
There are people sleeping on the ground.
Children playing in the street,
Are hungry 'cause there's nothing to eat.

Waste thrown out by you and me,
Is now being dumped into the sea.
And all the fish swimming by,
Are very quickly starting to die.

Countries warring day and night,
This dreadful killing just isn't right!
We shouldn't be fighting with each other,
But be in peace with one another.

Animals are being shot,
Some parts are taken then left to rot.
For some, this is a great, great sport,
Really, they should be taken to court.

And all of this we can change,
Our lives we must just re-arrange.
To solve the problem we're faced,
We'll have to recycle and not waste!

We must save the wildlife here,
And stop polluting the atmosphere.
Governments help to stop the war,
There'll be so much left to help the poor.

Heidi Christen (11)
Springvale House, Zimbabwe

Let's Go Green

Deforestation makes me so upset,
Our trees are special, to them we're in debt,
If you cut them down, where'll the creatures go?
Maybe they've young, how do you know?

Come on you people, let's pick up this litter,
Leaving this world looking more sweet than bitter.
Please stop the trees from being cut down,
Making our world more country than town!

All those huge factories giving out smoke,
With all this bad air, wouldn't *you* choke?
Don't we want to leave this place clean,
Come on everyone, let's all go green!

Poor little bears being shot for their skin,
Is it just for comfort, committing this sin?
Let's all think about our recycling,
I hope you all know it's a very good thing!

Becky Van Heerden (12)
Springvale House, Zimbabwe

Eco-Troubles

In this troubled world of ours
Much is unclean
Much is unfair
And seldom is anything ever shared.

Seeing people on the street
It almost makes me want to shed a tear!
Cold, homeless, and all alone
No one to love, they live in fear!

Animals are killed, they're being shot
Is it for their snuggly fur?
Or just for pleasure, or selfish comfort
I ask myself why this is so?

In the world that exists today
There is racism, war and poverty
People are being thrown onto the streets
Because they vote for a different party.

But in the world of bright tomorrow
We can work against these troubles
And that world will come sooner
If we all join hands and work together!

Tanya Chasara (11)
Springvale House, Zimbabwe

Helping The Homeless

Every day I watch as the homeless go by,
I look in their eyes and there's no hope.
They wish to be like some of us,
Their lives are never filled with splendour,
And yet, we are selfish and never think about them.
In the morning they have no bath,
During the afternoon they have no play,
And at night they have no shelter.
So let us lend a hand or at least a dollar!

Tatenda Jakaza (11)
Springvale House, Zimbabwe

Dealing With My Rubbish

Factories, cars, revolting stuff,
All these things have been used enough!
Fossil fuels are burning a lot,
How can we help this stuff to stop?

Rubbish is floating everywhere,
These days people don't seem to care!
Litter is just being thrown all around,
Rubbish is scattered all over the ground!

Forests are being cut down more,
My head is aching, it's feeling sore,
Human needs get bigger each day,
The world's being squeezed, what can it say?

I'll stop my litter on the floor,
Plant some trees, more and more!
Let's use our legs instead of cars,
Stop rockets going up to Mars!

It's our job to keep the world clean,
Turn our world from brown to green,
Let's stop polluting our fresh clean air,
Make life for Man and animals fair.

Nicola Baker (12)
Springvale House, Zimbabwe

The World In My Eyes

Seeing the world through my eyes,
Hearing the poor children's cries,
Knowing that they're cold and oh so hungry,
No one to help them, in bondage, not free.

Fearful eyes filled with tears,
Looking at me, terrified, but no one hears.
Screams surround me for help and love,
Imploring God for help from above.

The world of tomorrow we'll make a better place,
There is no white or black, we are all the same race.
Everyone to a family, no one alone,
No one to be poor, no one to groan.

How do we prevent the greenhouse affect?
How to look after the animals we protect?
The world is faced with problems so bad,
Much goes on that makes me sad!

We'll make our fields so green and bright,
So people aren't hungry from sun-up to night,
Let all people be forever keen,
Enjoying the advantages of a world so green!

Jordaan Hofmeyr (12)
Springvale House, Zimbabwe

Eco - Wars In The World

As I listen every day to the news
The things I hear are not those you would choose.
Hunger, wars, droughts and pollution
Leave many countries in destitution.
Children become all skin and bone
Away from home, left all alone.

While some wake up to a peaceful day
Some flee the war that's on its way.
Chances of surviving are very rare
For people in countries everywhere.
The world is making itself so desperate
By being just so inconsiderate!

Together we can make our world safe and mild
For every creature and every child.
'How do you do this?' You may well ask
Simply do your helpful task!
Recycling and consideration is one solution
To keeping this world free from pollution!

Miriam Gunda (12)
Springvale House, Zimbabwe

Worlds Dying In Front Of Us

Deforestation for the nation
So Man could have more transportation.
Highways and cars will cause pollution,
It seems too far gone for a solution.

Food prices are rising every day
Starvation and poverty are here to stay.
How to make the world a better place,
It's up to us, whatever our race!

Let's ensure food for animals is plenty
With dams and rivers never empty,
Stopping fuel pollution is a must
But in Africa electric cars would cause a fuss!

We need to stop wars within our own country,
And try to be tolerant of everyone you see.
The rich and the poor can work together
To make our world a living pleasure!

Jed Bromwell (11)
Springvale House, Zimbabwe

Eco-Poverty

All the smiles fade away.
All the laughter was yesterday.
I cannot buy that special toy.
I cannot feel any more joy.

Misery is now my life's perfect theme.
Wealth is a 'never come true' dream.
My choices now are so limited.
From other's company I am now omitted.

A life of abject poverty.
It's just a real tragedy!

No one wants to be close to me,
Because disgust is all they see.
I no longer have any friends,
It's like my life has come to an end.

A life of abject poverty.
It's just a real tragedy!

When we think of all the others.
When we help our sisters and brothers,
Poverty doesn't go any further,
Poverty's extinct, and our world's much brighter.

Ngoni Zinyama (12)
Springvale House, Zimbabwe

Our World

In our world, not all is right,
Littering, pollution and wars we fight.
Our deodorants contain CFCs,
But in a clean world we could be.

So much litter lying everywhere,
But there's a bin just over there.
People excrete in rivers, in dams,
Streams clog up with bottles and cans.

Cars driving along the street,
The latest ones are pretty neat!
But can you believe these things so cool,
Are burning very poisonous fuel.

Animals die this hunting season,
Wiped out for this pathetic reason.
Men kill animals just for fun,
Just for something to be done.

But we can change all this, we can!
Dredge the litter from the dam!
Use the bin and not the ground,
Then nature will sing, all around.

Jordan Taylor (11)
Springvale House, Zimbabwe

Rainforest, The Kaleidoscope

Rush! Listen to the steps of the forest, cracking twigs and leaves,
Something moves, somewhere, somehow.
So silent with no wind and life,
So gloomy, for the trees hide light.
Yet so noisy and crowded with toucans and macaws,
The rainforest is a kaleidoscope.

Rush! Listen to the wind's rustle as it swishes from treetop to treetop,
The rain falling gently and cold, to drench the ground's thirst.
Full of animals and plants together in harmony,
In a circle, a cycle in which they are all connected.
One huge living thing beating together,
The others are affected if one of them disappears.
The rainforest is a kaleidoscope.

But unfortunately not all is good,
If we insist on destroying and killing,
The capybaras will swim no more in the polluted rivers
And the macaws won't sing in cages,
Monkeys never again will giggle on their branches,
For we will have killed them all in no mercy for the trees.
The rainforest is a kaleidoscope.

Shall we continue with this unfair murder?
For the trees and animals haven't done anything to us.
How can we protest against such a thing?
And more importantly,
How can we make a difference?
Human greed and ambition are the problem,
Fight for your opinion,
The rainforest won't survive without your help.
A mixture of sadness, colour and beauty,
Will again be freed for life to spread again.

The rainforest is a kaleidoscope.

Louise Rodriges Lopes Vincent (11)
The British School Rio de Janeiro, Brazil

What's The Name

Oh, what's the name again,
Of the thing that was born perfect?
What's the name once more,
Of the thing that lives and gives life?

Sometimes it's sad and cries,
So its tears fall from the heavens.
Occasionally it's annoyed at us
And we hear its angry screeches.

Yet you can't remember,
I'll give you another chance,
We should treat it more tenderly,
I'll grant you one last chance.

It may even destroy buildings,
Or kill people, without pity,
But that's the time to think,
Do we treat it with pity?

Because every tree that falls
And every animal that dies, we will all suffer the consequence,
In a small amount of time.

So look even closer, can you remember the name
Of all these wonderful features?
If not, what a shame,
Oh, I've remembered . . . Nature.

Fernanda Coachman Figueira (12)
The British School, Rio de Janeiro

A World Of Difference - Poems From The UK And Around The World

Young Writers Information

We hope you have enjoyed reading this book - and that you will continue to enjoy it in the coming years.
If you like reading and writing poetry drop us a line, or give us a call, and we'll send you a free information pack.
Alternatively if you would like to order further copies of this book or any of our other titles, then please give us a call or log onto our website at www.youngwriters.co.uk

Young Writers Information
Remus House
Coltsfoot Drive
Peterborough
PE2 9JX
(01733) 890066